STOP T

l a Mills

CONTENTS

Introdution

Overthinking simply refers to thinking excessively, as the word suggests. In actuality, overthinking occurs when you choose to think more often than act or engage in other activities. If, instead of acting, you find yourself analysing, commenting, and repeating the same thoughts, you may be overthinking. This kind of unproductive behaviour can impede your success.

No two people overthink in the same manner, and each person will experience it in a unique way. But in general, overthinkers will concur that their inability to restrain their unfavourable emotions and thoughts has diminished the quality of their lives. Because their minds spend so much time and energy on one particular topic, people with these habits find it extremely difficult to interact, be productive at work, or enjoy hobbies. Such unrestrained emotions can be extremely detrimental to a person's mental health.

You will find it difficult to interact with them because you are overly preoccupied with what to say or what to do to keep the conversation going, which makes it harder to make new friends and keep them. Overthinking also makes it more difficult to maintain existing friendships. Even in a typical setting, it may be difficult for some people who are affected by this disease to engage in casual discussions or socialise with others. Additionally, some people could struggle to keep a commitment or visit the store. This way of thinking wastes time and depletes your energy, which keeps you from acting or discovering new possibilities. Furthermore, it impedes life advancement. This is comparable to putting a chain around your waist that is attached to a pole and running in circles; you will be busy but not productive. Making poor decisions will be impossible if you overthink everything.

You are more prone to feel frightened, worried, and out of your mind in such situations. You will be more successful, content, and have more peace of mind, nevertheless, when you quit overthinking.

Chapter 1: Overthinkign Disorder Defined

Definition of Overthinking

What precisely is overthinking? Overthinking syndrome is defined by experts as spending a lot of time thinking about everything and everything, which results in tension, fear, restlessness, concern, dread, unease, and many other negative emotions. This mental disorder impacts a person's capacity to work and complete daily chores since it involves more than just thinking about things too much. It also involves spending more time thinking about things.

No matter what you are thinking about, it may bother you for a moment before you go on to other aspects of your life. If you worry about your friends, your career, your family, your boyfriend and girlfriend, your life, and anything else, you may not believe that you have an overthinking condition. Yes, you occasionally come back inquisitive. You don't wonder about it all the time, though, and it doesn't interfere with your daily life. But when you have this kind of mental illness, all you can imagine is the troubled. Even if you aren't constantly and continuously concerned by the same issue, you worry about something.

You may encounter one or more of the following situations to determine whether you are overthinking everything:

- Difficulty in participating in and following a discussion.
- Constantly comparing yourself to people around you and how you stack up to them.
- Spending a lot of time thinking about the worst-case situations affecting family members or yourself.
- Reliving past mistakes and failures so frequently that you are unable to move over them.
- Reliving a past terrible event, such as the death of parents or other family members, abuse, which renders you incapable of handling it?
- Worrying excessively about your goals, dreams, or upcoming responsibilities until they become impossible to accomplish?
- Inability to control the flow of hazy ideas, feelings, and worries

No two people will experience this type of mental condition in the same manner. However, those who do experience overthinking will discover that their way of life and way of life are in jeopardy. This is because they are unable to effectively and efficiently control their negative emotions and ideas. They thus struggle to mingle and hang around. They also struggle to enjoy their hobbies and side jobs. They are not inventive or helpful in work. All of these occur as a result of their mind focusing inconsistent amounts of time and energy on different lines of thought. The belief that one does not have total control over their emotions or thinking can be very harmful to one's mental health.

With this mental illness, it's difficult to make acquaintances, meet up with people, and maintain friendships because you don't want to interact with them. You'll find it challenging to communicate with those around you. This occurs because you cause too much trouble with your actions and words. Additionally, you worry far too much about what will occur or how you will proceed. If you, your friends, or any family member suffers from this mental disease, you may find it difficult to engage in casual conversation with others. Additionally, it will be challenging to interact in a usual situation. It may be quite difficult for you to leave the house to go to the store or to your appointment, which has an impact on your entire life.

The truth is that practically every part of your life could be impacted by severe mental illness. Additionally, this may alter both your performance and how you interact with other people. Additionally, it may have an impact on your social life, job life, and, of course, your romantic life.

It can wreck your connection with your significant other, the relationships you have with others, and your entire way of life. Overthinking is a challenging disorder. It could lead to issues in your life.

Overthinking is a disorder that can strike anyone at any time. It can also turn into overthinking chaos if you have anxiety or any other type of anxiety illness. Your stress and anxiety over various life situations can easily turn into overthinking. You need to consider what you must do or how you can prevent unpleasant things from happening. You cannot prevent horrible and terrible things from happening, and that is a fact. Additionally, you are powerless to stop yourself from making every wrong choice. So, the best course of action is to seek help from friends, family, and experts.

Do you obsess over even seemingly minor details? Are you a chronic worrywart? Perhaps you naturally believe that if you worry or wonder enough, you can stop unpleasant things from happening. However, the truth is that worrying and wondering can impact your body in a variety of surprising ways. It can cause emotions of extreme tension and perhaps result in a dangerous health condition to overthink everything or worry excessively.

The Causes of Overthinking

Overanalyzing is a sign that you are bothered by anything. Identify the source of your agitation and deal with it right now. You can purge your thoughts by meditating. You can effectively and clearly organise, prioritise, and evaluate in your thoughts with this. Once the problem is identified, you may start working on a solution. This can help prevent you from getting caught up in a variety of unrelated and bad thoughts.

Mental Clutter Explained

- A never-ending list of "what ifs" and "shoulds" - all the things that need to be done - constitutes mental clutter.
- Regret the missed opportunities from the past.
- scared of potential future events
- Unfinished business, unanswered calls, unfinished emails, and unpaid bills
- People develop habits of complaining and critiquing, which deplete our physical and mental energies.
- In an effort to achieve perfectionism, criticise yourself when you fall short of your objective.

High levels of stress are caused by mental clutter, and stress is the main factor in overthinking, which can result in a number of health problems. As a result, you can:

Eliminate the need to complete tasks by switching from should to could. Give people the choice of doing it or not. A subtle shift in vocabulary can have an uplifting effect.

Past is past. It cannot be altered. Make a greater vision for your prospect by focusing your strength and efforts there.

Get started and schedule time to complete outstanding tasks and eliminate bothersome mental to-do lists.

Give up being disturbed and start doing something useful and entertaining. Not only does worrying waste time, but it can also deplete your vitality.

Cut off unhealthy behaviours and speak only on the positive aspects of your life.

Let go of the pressure to be faultless—who cares? possibly just you!

Here are some quick, simple, and useful strategies to help you organise your thoughts:

- The famed American poet Bill Copeland once said, "The difficulty with not having a goal is that you might spend your life running up and down the field and never score. Setting priorities is a wise strategy to proactively take charge of your life. You must first be aware of the things that are important to you, your life goals, and your long-term dreams. Make a list of your main priorities, and make sure that your actions and decisions represent those priorities. Second, make an action plan to accomplish your goals and figure out how to divide your time so that you can focus on each item on your list. It is critical to keep in mind that as you become older, your list of priorities may alter. That is acceptable as long as you constantly assess your needs to ensure that your priorities are beneficial to you.

- Journaling: Organizing and examining your thoughts in a journal is a wise method to relax your mind. One investigation was published in the Journal of Experimental Psychology: Writing in general and with purpose reduces intrusive negative thoughts and improves working memory. The gains, according to experts, may free up your cognitive resources for other intellectual tasks, such as the ability to manage anxiety more effectively. Because journaling is a great way to release bottled up emotions, it can also help with stress management and dealing with melancholy and depression. A journal can be created by anyone; you don't have to be an endless writer. The easiest method to use to begin with is bullet journaling.

- Knowing How to Free: Love yourself, accept who you are, and keep working toward your objectives. To soar to new heights Give up anything that is keeping you from reaching new heights. There is a passage in Roy T. Bennett's book The Light in the Heart that states, "It is crucial to break free of the negative feelings and thoughts that make you feel melancholy and sad." Eliminating unneeded worries, issues, concerns, and fears can reduce stress, boost self-esteem, and free up brain space. Check your thoughts every day, and make an effort to replace negative thoughts with constructive ones.
- Multitasking Is Not Beneficial: It sounds counterproductive to multitask. It is useless to prepare for an office presentation while simultaneously checking your Facebook account and looking for the ideal gift for your pals online. Multitasking is harmless as long as it's done occasionally. Your attention span is limited, stress levels are increased, and additional clutter is created since it is difficult for the brain to sort through irrelevant information when you are constantly switching between tasks. According to a Stanford University study, multitasking seriously reduces performance and may harm your cognitive control. So, the best course of action is to

finish each duty separately. Make a list of the tasks that must be completed first on that particular day. Make sure your list is straightforward and practical. Start with the most important thing.

- Take a Breath: Inhale deeply for a long time. Stop. Release gradually. Do it once more. It feels what? Not bad, huh? Deep breathing is a relatively easy but effective way to clear your mind.
- Additionally, this immediately promotes serenity and mood elevation. Additionally, it decreases your heart rate and blood pressure while stimulating the parasympathetic nerve system, which is crucial for maintaining your body's ability to rest. This activity not only relieves stress but also increases focus and fortifies your immune system.
- Make a choice: Professional organiser Scott Roewer claimed that clutter is simply a result of postponed decisions. If you consistently put off making decisions, the mess those postponed decisions create can eventually take over your thoughts. So stop putting it off and make that decision now. It makes no difference if it's about the new house you intend to buy or the call you've been putting off for so long. When making a straightforward choice, carefully weigh the benefits and drawbacks and never go back once

you've made your choice. Try the WRAP approach when making a crucial decision. This novel strategy is covered by the Heath brothers in Decisive: How to Make Better Decisions in Life and Work.

- Share Your Thoughts and Emotions with Friends and Family: A great technique to let go of suppressed and unspoken emotions is to discuss your problems with close friends or family members. In order to see things from a fresh viewpoint and think more clearly and wisely, it might be really helpful to share opinions.
- Limit media consumption: The impact of media on mental health is enormous. Many people spend a lot of time online and on their social media accounts. Reading blogs, watching trending videos, creating Pinterest boards, and other activities take up more of their time. Your brain may become blocked by this abundance of information, which can result in tension and anxiety. In order to clear your mind of media-related clutter, you must limit your use of social media. Start by establishing a limit. You should also choose which media you consume carefully. Avoid hazardous stuff at all costs. For the latest news and updates, only pay attention to reliable and trustworthy media

sources. Don't forget to check your inbox every day.

- Take Some Time to Unwind and Relax: Taking a break can help you clear your mind. Your body and mind both require time to rest and recharge if you want them to work properly. Therefore, put your phone and laptop away and focus on activities that will make you happy and grin. It doesn't matter if it's a protracted nap or a quick stroll through the playing field.

So, what clumsy feelings and ideas are still running through your head? The time has come to get rid of that garbage once and for all.

Social Expectation

Today's world is more demanding and difficult than ever to live and work in. Yes, we have modern conveniences that make life more comfortable and convenient, but we also have to deal with societal structure and expectations that we will follow a calendar that goes something like this: education, more school, entry-level career, climb the ladder, senior-level career, retirement.

This was the standard for those residing in economically powerful nations for a very long period. But a lot has changed in the last few decades, and it has done so at an exponentially faster rate. It's getting harder and harder to find a job in a lucrative field that will be fulfilling and pleasurable for thirty years or more. Along with the astonishing growth in human population and technological innovation, the rivalry has increased. Many of the occupations that were easily accessible to our parents are no longer around, and nowadays, asking for an employment application in person rather than applying online would draw peculiar looks. If you are successful in landing your desired career right out of high school or college, the real test of your mettle will begin. We could discuss office politics, rivalry, and competition all day long, but let's concentrate on some of the primary causes of overthinking in two of life's most significant contexts: work and education.

Let's continue our discussion of the difficulty of locating meaningful job as a young adult in the current world by examining how overthinking might be involved.

As a result of globalisation, marketing and advertising strategies have taken over the world. You've been warned that you will be up against numerous applicants, many of whom may be more qualified than you, from the very beginning of your career. Candidates are challenged during the interview process to present a strong case for why they should be chosen over the competition. You may do some practise at home in front of a mirror or brainstorm all the questions that might be asked. This is the point where you might begin to consider how you stack up against others in your industry. You recently earned a degree from college, feeling as though the world was at your feet and that a myriad of opportunities awaited you (best case scenario, of course). After a few months pass, you begin to understand that the job market is a little more competitive than you had anticipated and that you haven't yet shown that you are a lock for some of your ideal employers who have previously rejected you. Many young individuals in the millennial age can speak to the difficulties of graduating in the midst of the US economy's recession and struggling to land even the most rudimentary of jobs, never mind one that would launch a prominent career in their areas.

If and when things don't go as planned during your time in school, the pressure of the social expectation that you can and will get a fantastic career if you are smart and work hard enough becomes a heavy load. You could start to question yourself at this point and wonder if you have a flaw or a weakness that is preventing you from achieving your goals.

Contrary to what your parents or professors may have told you, there are a lot of elements that come into play when it comes to finding or getting your "dream job," and sometimes just working hard and having a happy attitude aren't enough. This is why many young adults start the cycle of overthinking that is driven mostly by issues of inadequacy and self-worth. I've failed and there is something wrong with me if society says I should be here or there at this stage in my life.

Once this conviction takes hold, it becomes very difficult to ignore the plethora of images, slogans, and advertisements that are all around us and show the ideal professional man or woman in their nice corner offices, dressed in the newest trends, sharing how they've made it this far because they work for this or that company, attended this or that school, purchased this or that car, purchased a house in this or that city, etc. At this point, you can start comparing your achievements to those of others, which only serves to fuel feelings of inferiority and low self-worth.

But let's imagine you've now secured a respectable position. Although it's not your ideal position, it could be a solid beginning for your career. It's your turn to shine right now. You turn to look at your peers, boss, and coworkers to determine where you are in the hierarchy of importance and how you compare to your rivals. Depending on the personalities around you, you can experience a lot of pressure to succeed and advance within the organisation. Because we are raised to believe that being the greatest is the only way to advance in your organisation, work life quickly becomes a contest. As you continually assess how well you perform your duties, this strain may appear as daily overthinking. Everyone wants to do a good job in their job, therefore in and of itself, this is not a terrible thing. When we start constantly comparing ourselves to others and when working becomes a competitive race to the top rather than a setting where like-minded individuals collaborate to improve the firm, a problem occurs.

Once you've made it to the pinnacle of business society, the rivalry shifts to rival businesses in your industry—eclipsing their market, forcing rivals out of business, etc. Furthermore, everyone is familiar with the adage "the more you acquire, the more you have to lose." As you calculate how far you might fall if you make a mistake or go off the ladder, this creates a whole new source of concern and overthinking.

Could it be you? Do you worry about your professional standing all the time? Perhaps you are underemployed and feel ashamed because you feel like you haven't progressed in life enough when you look at other people. Although this may be one of the most frequent causes of overthinking, it's time to go back in time to look at how social expectations form in young children. Let's examine the social norms in school.

Most of us aren't truly considering life after school while we're young. While we might have some fantastical ideas floating about in our heads, the most of the time we just want to know what mom brought for lunch and whether or not that big child will push us off the swing at recess one more today. (Ideally not; yet, you get the idea.)

Social pressure and expectations take on a more urgent importance in our lives as we get older and attend middle school and high school. While we may have distant thoughts about our future careers, the majority of us are worried about things like whether or not we'll get a date to the dance, how popular we are at school, etc. At this age, a lot of societal pressure is focused on academic or competitive success, as well as physical appearance. Sadly, most girls at this age start to obsess about their physical beauty and may even start to believe that it determines their worth. When these women look around at the stunning ladies on social media and in magazines, they start comparing themselves to those unachievable goals, which serves as the catalyst for overthinking. Similar to young girls, young boys may look up to a sports role model or even a father figure who has achieved great success in his work and start comparing themselves to males, attributing their self-worth to success in academic achievement, popularity, or competitive sports.

If you choose to go to college, the pressure will only increase as you start. Many students struggle to balance their social and academic lives, which leads to their dropping out of college. The entry into the world of professional work, where a brand-new set of social pressures and expectations awaits, is made possible by maintaining focus, getting those much-desired bachelor's degree, and maintaining good grades.

As you can see, a large portion of our overthinking may originate from a skewed perception of who we are in relation to others in our social or professional situations. As we are continually inundated with pictures and messages in the media determining what success should look and feel like, this pressure starts early in life and persists.

Let's examine some additional potential causes of overthinking.

Afraid of Failure

Most individuals are familiar with the concept of failure fear. In actuality, most of us are driven to work hard by this. You discover that you are motivated by your internal dread rather than striving hard for a promising future.

Unimportant choices

Sometimes we force ourselves to make decisions that are not necessary, and as a result, we end up making useless choices. For instance, there are times when we wind up making decisions that are irrelevant based on assumptions while we are thinking about the future. For instance, you might assume that you must get married since you are growing older if you take marriage as an example.

Afraid of What the Future Holds

The frightening future is another factor. The thoughts of what might or might not happen frequently occupy your mind when you overthink the future. You can find yourself worrying a lot about things that, when you think about it, are unlikely to happen. However, your thoughts are racing and you're preoccupied with dire implications.

In the present, procrastination can manifest as delaying a decision for an excessive amount of time. You could find yourself hesitating when deciding what to say or do. Then, before you realise it, your chance has already passed, leaving you with nothing but regret over the chance you wasted due to your inaction.

For instance, you've been given the opportunity to transfer to a different city in order to accept the job of your dreams. You naturally want to do your homework and research the new city and business. Thoughts about how little you know about the new work, though, paralyse you. You worry excessively about acting improperly. Then, you reflect on earlier circumstances where you might have made a poor decision. Soon, you become so reluctant to respond that you are unable to get the courage to say "yes" or "no." In the end, the employer decided to hire someone else because of your lack of initiative.

Therefore, spending too much time overthinking, getting caught up in the past, or worrying excessively about the future may cause you to miss out on the fantastic opportunities that life has in store for you RIGHT NOW.

Again, there is nothing wrong with considering your issues so that you may come up with a solution; the difficulty arises when you have a poor habit of turning stories around in your head until you can see every angle and side to them. Overanalyzing is counterproductive since it causes you to obsess over your issues without trying to find a solution and only serves to make you feel miserable.

You must determine the root reason of your tendency of overthinking in order to come up with a workable solution to end it. Here are some of the more frequent explanations for why people frequently overthink their issues rather than actually coming up with a solution.

Overload with information

When you lack confidence, you often second-guess everything you say and do. You are allowing doubt and fear to seep into your head when you pause, even just a little, about the things you want to achieve. Once they are in, it will be very challenging to get them out. You can never fully predict where your choices will lead you; even if you meticulously arrange every last detail, the results will still fall short of your expectations (it could either be better or worse than what you planned). Because of this, you should learn to take chances and stop punishing yourself when your efforts do not yield the desired outcomes.

When You Worry Too Much

It is only normal to worry when you come into fresh and strange situations. However, worrying excessively will cause you to overthink if you are unable to even envision a favourable conclusion. This is a problem because worrying draws in additional issues and, occasionally, generates ones out of thin air, which leads to deeper overthinking. Consider thoughts that are more optimistic, such as how much better you would feel if something goes your way, rather than dwelling on how things might go wrong.

When You Overthink to Protect Yourself

Some individuals assume that when they overthink, they can shield themselves from problems, but in reality, overthinking is a trap that prevents you from moving forward. Stifling your growth is never a good thing at all, even while it may appear beneficial to overthink things and do nothing to alter the status quo. Additionally, when you overthink, you are essentially reversing any progress you have already made. Instead of staying in the same place.

You are Unable to "Turn Off" Your Mind

Many people who tend to overthink do so because, despite their best efforts, they can never seem to take their thoughts off of their problems. People who are vulnerable to stress appear to be perpetually wound up; they have lost the ability to unwind and interrupt their train of thinking. When a person concentrates too much on a particular issue and is unable to shift his attention away from it, overthinking occurs.

You are Always Chasing after Perfection

Perfectionist tendencies are not always a good thing. In actuality, it may be argued that being a perfectionist is not at all beneficial. The majority of perfectionists experience ongoing anxiety. They frequently awaken in the middle of the night contemplating the things they could have done more effectively. Overthinking results from being a perfectionist since you are constantly attempting to surpass yourself.

Overthinking is Your Habit

Sometimes overthinking is the person's poor habit rather than being the cause of their bad habits. It doesn't take much for some people to overthink; they typically do so the instant they experience even a slight difficulty. People are unable to live their life the way they really want to because of this unhealthy habit.

Fear

If you don't confront the worries that are the source of your worry, it will never go away entirely. You can only feel powerful after you have control over your dread and apprehension feelings, which you can only do if you confront your fears head-on.

Make a note of everything you are frightened of doing after learning how to regulate your negative thoughts and pay attention to how you feel. You can include anything you believe is holding you back on that list, such as telling your crush how you really feel, starting your own business, getting your book published, exploring adventure sports, and so on.

Once your list is complete, choose any one fear that you would like to conquer initially and design a strategy to defeat it. Prepare a brief speech about a subject you are passionate about and practise giving it for a minute or two in front of a mirror, a close friend, or by yourself if you are shy about public speaking but have always wanted to do it.

Speak on the subject in front of two to three people once you have control of it. You might falter and make mistakes, but if you can maintain your composure during that period, you will partially conquer your fear. Continue speaking in front of more people gradually, and you will eventually be able to face your fear.

Take on another small fear after conquering the first one, and then another. To better manage your emotions and have more control over them, keep battling your anxieties in this manner and thwart them one at a time. In order to review the accounts repeatedly, keep track of your daily activities and performance in a notebook. This provides insight into your triumphs, weaknesses, blunders, and failures, motivating you to recognise your successes, learn from your errors, and correct them going forward.

Chapter 2: How to Clean Up Your Thoughts

How to Quit Stressing

We all worry occasionally. You constantly worry about both yourself and other people. To some extent, this is typical. You can be concerned about the possibility of failure, your safety, or other potential problems. Since animals must worry about their hunger until they eat for themselves, it is innate. Worrying is unhealthy, though, to a certain extent. You need to take action if you worry all the time to the point that it controls your life. Life must be enjoyable for you. While having occasional worries is inevitable, they shouldn't keep you from carrying out your daily activities. When worry becomes out of control, it needs to be addressed.

You must develop the ability to relax. There is always a chance that something bad will happen, but you need to be able to focus on the good instead of always worrying about what might go wrong. You need to be able to enjoy yourself in the now rather than obsessing over what you did wrong in the past or what might go wrong in the future. You need to be able to appreciate life instead of living it in constant stress. It's crucial to learn how to put an end to "what-ifs" and cultivate the ability to concentrate on the ideal outcome. You need to be able to strike a healthy balance between being practical and being upbeat. You should also learn to recognise your own feelings.

Stop Worrying

Just quit worrying—that sounds easy enough. It is possible to train your brain to become less anxious and more able to have fun, despite the fact that this may seem easier said than done. You can significantly reduce your worry and even stop it from happening if you want to. But you'll need to practise a lot and be patient as you advance. If you have a natural tendency to worry, it will take some time to break this habit and replace it with healthier ones. To lessen the amount of worrying you do, you must be able to modify your mind.

You may cut down on the amount of time you spend worrying in a few different ways. To simply schedule time to worry is one approach. Set aside time each day to just let your emotions happen rather than repressing your problems and ignoring them until they become too much for you to handle. Allow yourself to experience everything without opposing it. Even seeing yourself overreacting will help you understand how helpful—or detrimental—letting your emotions rule can be. You'll benefit from setting aside some time each day to just let it all out. You can either opt to record everything verbatim or keep a journal. Maybe you type out everything you think and then delete it so you can see a clearing of your thoughts right there in front of you. You can decide to open out to someone you trust and let yourself rant for a while to let everything out. In any case, expressing your feelings rather than repressing them is beneficial.

Find the cause of your concerns. It's possible that you're overscheduling yourself and need something to keep your thoughts occupied. To keep yourself occupied, you may decide to pick up a pastime. It's possible that a specific incident causes your anxieties. While looking through social media, you could start to feel anxious as you compare yourself to others and worry that you aren't good enough. Perhaps a past trauma from which you haven't yet recovered is the cause of your fears. Whatever the reason, it's crucial to take some time to consider your worries and come up with a solution.

If your concerns are manageable or not is another factor to take into account. If the worry can be resolved, find a way to do it and implement it. Solve it so that you can feel more at ease rather than ruminating on it. You have to be ready to acknowledge worries that you can't fix. Accept the uncertainty rather than trying to forecast the worst or stressing about unlikely possibilities. Will worrying make it better or worse? The most likely response is "no." Being anxious won't stop bad surprises.

You must be prepared to acknowledge that life is continuously changing. You can be happy and experience less stress by looking for the positive aspects of these changes.

Live in the Moment

You can actually quit worrying by developing the ability to live in the now. Worry is frequently a reaction to the past or future. Usually, we don't worry as much about what we are doing right now. You must be prepared to let the past go and live without looking back. Every setback will only make you stronger because it is an opportunity to learn. Since the future is uncertain, the best you can do is put up your best effort to shape it into the future you desire. However, it's hard to do that when you're constantly worried!

If you can't learn to enjoy the moment, you'll never be able to enjoy life. Otherwise, you'll perpetually long for the past or dream of a better life in the future. But tomorrow never comes. Today is always the case. You must therefore understand the significance of living in the present. Be present-minded. Recognize all the good things that are happening right now. You might need to turn off your technological devices and pay close attention to your surroundings to do this. Be more mindful and take a moment to appreciate how wonderful the moment is. Accept your current ideas while allowing yourself to turn off those that are related to the past or the future. Get conscious of your senses. What are you noticing in terms of sight, sound, smell, feel, and taste? Instead of continually juggling multiple tasks, stop and enjoy what you are doing.

You could value life's smaller aspects. Be grateful for the little things and the things you may have overlooked in the past. Life is considerably more complex than what meets the eye. Your happiness can be greatly affected by even the tiniest things. Be grateful for everything, even the little things in life.

By being joyful and spreading happiness to others, you may live in the present. Do not forget to grin and laugh. These can significantly increase your happiness and make life more enjoyable for you. Additionally, spread joy to other people. Volunteering and carrying out little deeds of kindness can make a big difference. Knowing that you had a purpose and made a difference will make you pleased. Be grateful for everything you have and make an effort to assist anyone else who might be in need. Take a time now and again to reflect on all the things for which you are grateful. Try to be positive every day.

Spend a little time alone. You might decide to practise meditation. You can also just breathe and pay attention to your breath. Take some time to unwind and pay attention to how your body feels. You might think that you are too stressed out to appreciate the moment. Remind yourself to live in the moment on a frequent basis by checking in with yourself. It will take some deliberate effort at first because it is instinctive to think about the future or linger on the past. You will learn to enjoy life no matter what when you can live in the now.

Stop the "What-Ifs"

There are a lot of "what-ifs" that could happen. If you have a tendency to worry incessantly, you will inevitably think the worst. However, this way of thinking is useless. You won't have the drive to keep going if you consistently expect and assume the worse. Given that you anticipate the worst, you will feel as though there is no purpose in continuing. It is crucial that you break this cycle and adopt a positive outlook on life. Even though it's crucial to maintain realism, you can't always plan for the worse.

Being optimistic and realistic should coexist in harmony. You can't always get your hopes up for everything; having outrageously irrational expectations won't assist you since you'll feel let down all the time. You cannot, however, view life as meaningless and hold the belief that misfortune awaits you at every turn. You must be prepared to accept that life will be full of both difficulties and accomplishments, despite the fact that you might believe that this is more realistic. You miss out if you only concentrate on one. You will learn more about yourself, other people, and life in general via mistakes and adversity. The wonderful times wouldn't be as pleasant if life didn't have troubles. It's imperative to acknowledge that both of these will happen and that you must be prepared to accept the good with the bad. You'll be able to live a life that is less anxious and more joyful if you do this.

There are times when everyone has "what-if" thoughts. This is typical and beneficial for making decisions. When they begin to disrupt your routine, they may however cause harm to your daily life. You need to make adjustments to yourself regarding your worrying if you find it difficult to carry out your daily activities because you are too preoccupied with the possibility of negativity. It's problematic when you can't manage your thoughts.

You can use a few techniques to manage these ideas. One approach is to record these ideas as they come to mind. As a result, you will become more aware of your thoughts and may come to the realisation that they are illogical. You'll become more aware of your thoughts as a result, and you could even comprehend why you think the way you do. Additionally, you must to act on these ideas. If there is a solution to the issue you are concerned about, take it. Find a method to let rid of the thought if there isn't one. Speak to someone, put it in writing, or give it some thought. Take a minute to consider the notion, how it makes you feel, and how you are responding to it. This will enable you to react to it more emotionally and act appropriately to resolve the problem. Additionally, you must learn to be more at ease with change and uncertainty. Recognize that fretting won't change the result of some things; they will simply remain unknown until they happen.

Become More Aware of Yourself

Self-awareness can be very beneficial. It can greatly facilitate your ability to comprehend your feelings and experience more mental control. You'll come to understand the reasons behind your actions and thoughts. Your talents and limitations are clear to you. You'll also learn your motivations thanks to it. You'll become more conscious of your life's purpose and objectives. You might even find that it helps you communicate more effectively and better understand others. You will have a healthy mind and feel much better about yourself and your emotions if you increase your self-awareness.

You will initially need to make a conscious effort to increase your self-awareness. Spend some time every day seriously considering how you are feeling. Recognize your feelings as they arise, their origins, and how they affect you. You might also think back on the full day. Did you succeed in completing your goal? If not, why didn't you do it earlier? Take this opportunity to give yourself a helpful critique. Don't just focus on your shortcomings, judge yourself against others, or concentrate about how you failed. Instead, acknowledge what did and did not work for you. You will gain from doing this since you will be able to apply what you learn to the next day. At first, you won't be perfect, but if you can get better every day, you'll be considerably better off. Only evaluate yourself in relation to yesterday. You should continually grow, get better, and change for the better. This is a natural method to advance in life, and doing it will help you become the finest version of yourself. Remember to consider both what can be worked upon and what you did well, since it is crucial to keep in mind your accomplishments and the fact that success is possible for you.

There are various ways you might ask others to assist you. Talking out your feelings with someone you trust is one approach to do this. This can assist you in communicating your ideas verbally. Additionally, since they can offer you an opinion apart from your own, you are welcome to solicit input from others. But it has to be wholesome. You should believe what the other person says and make sure that you interpret everything they say as an opportunity to get better, not as a criticism of who you are as a person.

It's crucial that you can express your values and objectives in writing. You'll become more conscious of your goals as a result. You won't have direction or a sense of purpose in life if you don't have goals to work for. Recognize what matters to you and what makes you feel valuable. You cannot evaluate your progress towards obtaining your goals if you don't have any goals. You won't be able to monitor your progress as a result.

You can severely limit your potential by worrying. You will be spending your time worrying rather than enjoying life. It's imperative that you make an effort to reduce the amount of worrying you do as a result. You'll not only be happy but also less agitated and anxious. A burden will also be taken off of your shoulders. Instead of meditating on what doesn't matter, it will be simpler for you to concentrate on what does. You'll feel more important in life and be able to focus on the things that are important to you. You'll feel more competent to do your daily chores at work. You'll feel closer to your neighbours when you're at home. You will be able to conduct your day without feeling overtaken by worry while you are out and about.

There are a few ways you may work on your worrying habit, and it's crucial to break it. Thought must be given to the fact that stopping oneself from worrying will need effort. In order to appreciate life and feel happier, it's also crucial to learn how to live in the now. Stopping your own "what-ifs" can definitely help. You will feel better for not having these ideas, as the majority of them are needless. Finally, in order to worry less, you must increase your self-awareness.

Practicing Positive Mindfulness

Have you ever felt pressured by life, restless, or overwhelmed?

Our world is quite busy. You probably feel stressed out frequently since there are so many messages flying about as you are stepping on your children's toys and attempting to feed the dog when the food on the table is growing cold.

If you practise mindfulness regularly, you'll be able to reduce your anxiety and stress, reduce the amount of time you feel overwhelmed, and learn to appreciate each moment as it comes. Being mindful could very well be the trick you need to figure out how to have the flexibility to adjust to the frenzy in a world of chaos.

Fortunately, there is a simple tendency you can use to usually quiet yourself down and appreciate life more. It is known as mindfulness. The practise of mindfulness involves consciously focusing the majority of your attention on the present moment and accepting it without judgement. If you're looking for the essential ingredient in joy, this is a fantastic place to start.

If these sound like outcomes you'd like to get involved in, I advise reading this extreme guide to being cautious throughout the day. We'll start by discussing the benefits of mindfulness and how it can positively impact both your mental and physical well-being.

The Benefits of Mindfulness

Uncertainty decreases with mindfulness.

According to research, mindfulness is especially effective at reducing anxiety. Consistently practising mindfulness rewires your brain, enabling you to refocus your attention. You can learn how to see the truth about your thoughts and then let them go rather than chasing a stressful or unpleasant idea down a path to every possible outcome.

Mindfulness enhances recall, concentration, and performance.

One of the most important psychological skills a person can have is the ability to focus on the task at hand. One of the few techniques that can help you stop your mind from wandering and the detrimental effects that losing focus may have on you is mindfulness. The truth is that research on students has shown a connection between mindfulness and concentration throughout the study hall.

Additional research has shown that dwelling on a well-known idea thickens the cerebral cortex of the brain, which is responsible for memory, fixation, and understanding.

Practicing mindfulness relieves suffering.

Every day, almost 100 million Americans suffer the negative impacts of unrelenting suffering, but 40 to 70 percent of them do not receive appropriate medical care. Numerous studies have shown that mindfulness meditation can lessen pain without relying on endogenous narcotic mechanisms that are typically used to do so in subjectively based systems like mindfulness.

Self-made narcotic systems have typically been thought of as the key component of the mind for reducing pain without the need of drugs. Three narcotics, including beta-endorphin, met- and leu-enkephalins, and dynorphins, are self-produced by this system. Together, they practise mindfulness to minimise suffering.

Practicing mindfulness reduces emotional response

Being less really receptive is typically near the top of the list of the several reasons people frequently have for learning to meditate. Being cautious or "Zen" is compared to rolling with the punches in life and not being open to opportunities that may present themselves.

Additionally, there is undoubtedly something to this. Comparatively to a control group, mindfulness meditation has enabled study participants to detach their emotions from painful images and focus more on an intellectual task.

Rumination and excessive thinking are reduced by mindfulness.

Rumination or overthinking is one of the most well-known signs of tension. When you start to worry about anything, your mind will hold onto it tightly and make it challenging to let go. It is really easy to fall into an idea circle where you keep thinking about the worst-case scenario. We all understand that this is useless because worrying about something doesn't prevent it from happening.

One study showed that those who were new to mindfulness and began practising it during a retreat had the opportunity to display fewer signs of rumination and unease than the control group.

More happy connections result from mindfulness.

Scientists are still unsure how this occurs, but recent brain research has shown that those who practise mindfulness regularly exhibit both negative and beneficial alterations in the brain regions linked to enhanced sympathy, empathy, and giving.

The effects of mindfulness on the amygdala, the brain's eager planning centre, are another benefit. The amygdala's volume and its connection to the prefrontal cortex both decline in relation to mindfulness. This suggests that mindfulness may strengthen emotional rules and reduce reactivity, which are two crucial tools for creating and maintaining connections.

Consciousness enhances sleep

The pressing reaction is strikingly inversed by the relaxing response that your body needs to attentive reflection. This unwinding response aims to reduce a number of stresses brought on by medical issues, such as agony, wretchedness, and hypertension. These illnesses frequently come with sleep problems.

One study of more experienced adults confirms that practising mindfulness meditation can aid in achieving a good night's sleep. According to the results of this investigation, mindfulness meditation can increase the relaxation response by strengthening the attentional components that provide it control over the autonomic sensory system.

Some pressure is reduced through mindfulness.

People are frequently tortured with a great deal of worry because they are looked at with an expanding amount of weight today because of the mind-boggling character of our general public. This comes on top of a lot of other medical problems. By acting as a preventative measure, mindfulness can lessen anxiety while also assisting people in overcoming challenging situations.

The benefits of mindfulness for mental health

Integrative body-mind training, or IBMT, has been shown to initiate beneficial auxiliary changes in the brain that may protect against mental infection. This tactic supports productivity in a region of the brain that allows people to control their behaviour.

Mindfulness advances intellectual adaptability

One study suggests that mindfulness training may increase people's intellectual agility in addition to helping them become less responsive. According to all accounts, those who practise mindfulness are also prepared to exercise self-perception, which removes the neural connections created by past learning and enables understanding of current information in a different way.

Reflection also activates the area of the brain that is linked to flexible responses to pressure, which is comparable to a quicker return to a baseline line of thinking after being adversely influenced.

Mindfulness in Everyday Life

As we've already mentioned, mindfulness is a discipline that is not just for monks who have taken a vow of silence. Almost anyone can engage in this form of practise at any time and in any location.

So, here are some more methods to incorporate mindfulness into your daily life:

Sit with your experience

You can sit with your experience once you focus on exercising caution.

You can become even more in control by practising mindfulness while focusing on your body, mind, and spirit. The more often you do this, the more your sense of self will be blocked out, and you will feel better about yourself overall.

Focus on your relaxation when you close your eyes and relax. Watch out for nearby or even distant sounds. Get a sense of what is loose and what is holding strain by moving your body. If you get a tingle, acknowledge it without attempting to change it. Just move through it.

This is a terrific technique for just being cautious without trying to handle business.

Life can occasionally be awkward like a tingling. You can notice that things oscillate if you sit with the experience.

While you think, anxiety may creep up on you or you can feel a tightness in your throat.

The body is being informed that there are several activities by the brain. When you do experience tension in the body, you might put your hands inside that area and say, "This as well." You are fully acknowledging your understanding without seeking to change it. Being mindful in this way.

Assume you are sitting outside in a recreation area. Everything is well until you notice two people who are clearly in love. Suddenly, despair sets in, and no one is nearby to support the inclination. This feeling of disappointment has always been present in your heart.

Although it is not always present, it may do so at any time. Your body weakens, and you get a sinking sensation in your chest. Your memories of previous times when you felt lonely are triggered, and stored energy from the past strikes a chord.

Without phoning someone or using a dated equipment to quiet your thoughts and feelings, how would you handle the situation?

Basically, make sure your notes were taken. You are the thing being observed and the subject. Those feelings of emptiness are things. Find out who is experiencing the suffering and depression. Allow the emotions to run their course without running or avoiding them.

Being mindful does not entail appearing to display one's psyche. It has to do with fully acknowledging how the body, mind, and psyche are responding.

There will be times when the touchy part of you that has had many interactions will feel uneasy, poor, and desirous. Everything is affected by the intellect and conscience in this way. You are the watchful person and the intelligent inhabited entity.

Simply maintain 100 percent focus to benefit from the part of you that is watching out for this human experience.

For those who haven't practised mindfulness, everything I'm saying can seem quite confusing. To understand the technique I'm describing, you simply need to invest some time in not responding and instead paying attention to your experience.

Reflection is a fantastic technique to use during awkward moments.

Attempt this activity

Get to know the one in your head properly. Just inside, introduce yourself properly. Who introduces themselves properly and who says hello? You are the one listening in and speaking.

Stepping back is the best way to break free from the constant chatter that is supporting your horrifying beliefs. Take a cold, objective look at things. Musings are merely a psychological artefact that should be let to flow by rather than grasped or discounted.

If you pay close attention to the voice, you'll begin to realise that the majority of what it says is meaningless. It bemoans the past and makes use of previous interactions in an effort to exert control over more recent and upcoming ones. Numerous problems arise in your life as a result of this.

You need to be alert enough to carefully monitor what's going on in your head if you want to become liberated from it. When you realise that a lot of your actions are being driven by an absurd voice seeking solace, you can start to make other decisions.

Overall, mindfulness can fix a lot of things, but how do we go about doing that? Contemplation is one method for calming the mind and entering our own selves.

Everyday contemplation

Though contemplation isn't tough, many people feel threatened by its ease.

This is because you don't want to calm down your self-image. It signals to you that you're overly preoccupied, that contemplation is irrelevant, and that it's uncommon and alien for you in an overly extreme way.

In actuality, the self-image is scared of becoming at peace. There is the power to resist awkward sentiments by backing off and moving in different directions. By avoiding danger or distress, you gave yourself a sense of purpose.

There is a great risk of reliving past suffering when we are thinking.

You can finally control old injuries through your thinking so that you don't have to continue to live with them. That suggests that they will never again be able to control you.

You must regularly put in a lot of effort to develop mindfulness, but this shouldn't be a chore. The mind will chatter and let you know it is worn out. Just keep observing the thoughts and feelings that are passing through you.

The more you do it, the more eagerly you'll look forward to that uninterrupted alone time. Think of it as a daily back rub or trip to the spa. That focused disposition makes you feel as relaxed as spending 40 minutes in a sauna once you get into it.

The advantages will become more noticeable the more mindfulness you practise, however you'll start to see benefits almost immediately.

Reflection is a key component of mindfulness training in both modern psychotherapy and Buddhist thought.

Don't sit in lotus position and eat those incense sticks at this time; there are many different ways to reflect. There are many things you may do for your body, mind, and spirit when you reflect, which is the canopy for healing.

The practise of mindfulness contemplation has nothing to do with altering or changing yourself in any way. It is connected to learning to recognise your identity. You will experience things when you relax and sit. Recollections may surface as you dig deep inside of yourself, much like a movie playing on a screen.

You can learn a lot if you stay in the centre of awareness and avoid getting distracted. If you get sucked in, it will be obvious since you won't let the photographs go. You'll become genuinely involved, and tension will start to rise.

According to Buddha, trying to escape your current experience is the source of your enduring. It is akin to pieces of anguish to continue living in a nice moment from your past. In general, clutching objects keeps you before them and is detrimental to your mental health.

Meditation

We are told to avoid feeling anxiety and to choose convenience and immediate satisfaction over the difficult path. But those of us who ruminate frequently choose the difficult route. The stance of confidence is one of a puzzle, where we learn the audacity to believe in what we cannot see and the solidarity to let go of our fear of vulnerability.

Every time I enter a state of contemplation, it is an act of faith that brings me closer to reality by squeezing me into dread. I was able to search for that reality, to choose the more difficult road, and to continuously develop empathy for myself thanks to the act of contemplation.

Over the years, I've discussed a few different types of reflection that have aided me during some of the scariest periods of my life.

Qigong Meditation

Dread is acknowledged to be stored in the kidneys in Traditional Chinese Medicine. In Western medicine, it is understood that frightening symptoms are only chemical and electrical signals that are activated by a perplexing system of communication in the body's cells. Once such brain pathways are created and sufficiently reinforced, a comparable response occurs each time a threat is noticed.

Your feet should be level with the floor while you sit. Place both hands above the kidneys (at your back under your lower ribs). Imagine them and the little adrenal glands that are located above them.

The mind returns to those pathways to carry out identical actions whenever it perceives threat, whether real or imagined. Additionally, that is where qigong pondering comes into play. By repeating encouraging thoughts, you can strengthen your brain pathways, cleanse your kidneys, and give yourself more significant control over your emotions.

After a few breath cycles, bend slightly forward as you breathe in, tuck your hands behind your knees, open your eyes, and imagine exhaling fear while uttering the sound "choo."

Close your eyes, grinned, and imagined harmony and a dull blue glow around your kidneys and adrenal glands. Drive your stomach back in as you exhale.

Lean In

The act of reflecting is meant to be practical and to guide us as we move through our time with a touchstone of peace and mindfulness. Similarly, as with any emotion, reflection can help us become more balanced despite our apprehension so that we can understand it more clearly.

With growing intensity of reflection, you can empower yourself to face dread in an ever-more-positive way as the day goes on.

Regularly check in with your emotions. Let your negative feelings persist whenever they arise.

Instead of running, take a deep breath and approach your fears and anxieties with neighbourliness and interest. Be considerate of yourself in times of dread, just as you would a trusted friend.

If you have the time and room, sit down and take ten breaths while inhaling into your fear.

Dread as power

Dread is saying that the opportunity to perform what you're seeking to do is optimal right now. Your body is actually preparing you for a successful outcome. You can learn to control your fear if you genuinely understand that it is a feeling just like any other. Then you'll be able to accomplish things that the majority of others would consider outstanding.

I have learned to overcome my phobia of heights by enrolling in a lead shake climbing class, which requires me to climb to the top of the partition and mainly free fall down it before being caught with a rope.

I've learned how to breathe through the dread and let go repeatedly thanks to practise, openness, and supportive friends and teachers. The dread is still there, but how I react to it has altered.

What are you afraid of? Try it yourself. What safe, small steps could you take to try to disapprove of your breath in that fear? What modifications do you notice after some time of practise?

Positive energy can be used to manage your thoughts.

Although there are thousands of moments in a day, we only ever experience one at a time. As soon as we begin to alter this situation, our lives begin to alter as well. Do you tend to give things too much thought? Jamaica Hunt But what is overthinking really like? Rethinking is "too much, foolishly and passively thinking; continually pondering the significances, triggers and effects of your personality, your emotions and especially your issues," according to psychologists who have conducted substantial research in the topic. It can entail going to bed at night contemplating how awful the economy is, how useless my funds are, how likely it is that I will lose my job, and how unlikely it is that I will ever be able to send my kids back to college. Or it can entail repeatedly reflecting throughout the day on how ugly your fine, wispy hair is.

In her article on "How to avoid overthinking and start a life," Gail Blankets shared a storey about how she was fascinated by choosing the perfect outfit for the Financial Women's Association annual dinner in 2007, knowing that she would be meeting some very well-known and likely very good-looking women. She acknowledges that she had been considering it for days, even making lists and sketches of all the possibilities and attempting to dress appropriately, when all of a sudden her friend, who was 25 at the time, inquired, "Why are you working so hard?" "Business attire," reads the invitation. I keep thinking about it and I feel like "Does that imply that she finds my logic illogical? Or why didn't he respond to my email? That was sent three days ago. Is he angry for whatever reason? Is he punishing me? Am I not important enough to care?" Someone who frequently wonders why a friend or supervisor hasn't made eye contact with them or talked to them in a room sits down to feel awful and then doesn't think it's worthwhile making the effort or taking the risks required for high performance.

The majority of individuals believe that when they experience disappointment or depression, it will motivate them to reflect carefully and evaluate the problem in order to resolve it. The contrary is actually true when it comes to science. Constantly thinking about potential negative events has a tendency to make people worse rather than better. Yes, according to Lyubomirsky, there is ample evidence that repeatedly thinking about a sad or upsetting event is bad for us (also called "rumination"). It can be so detrimental that it keeps us from taking meaningful proactive actions to remedy the situation and can cause people who are vulnerable to experience an attitude decline, cynical reality distortion, and even clinical depression.

Problems abound in life and the environment you live in, ranging from tiny irritations, errors, and flaws to significant tragedies and terrifying dangers and possibilities. It doesn't magically make us more resilient to these technologies or more stable. In actuality, it worsens our feelings and reduces our likelihood of taking positive steps to change our attitudes or undo those changes.

There is none other than now, when people have little faith in the government and corporate America to provide the adequate, fair services, protections, and leadership required to keep the country running smoothly. This is a time of bad financial news, a volatile economy, and growing disillusionment with both.

How is it possible to disregard your career, your personal objectives, your family, and your relationships? You can get so depressed as a result of this that you refrain from taking chances, interacting with others, and putting up the necessary effort to succeed. Being there for the people that mean to you the most might be difficult and even stressful. Ultimately, rethinking can sap the optimism necessary to work hard, speak up, and disseminate positive ideas due to its predictions of certain failure and awful consequences.

Have you ever carried it out? How can you put a stop to it?

Tips for coaching:

1. Use proven strategies to lessen and prevent overthinking. Surprisingly, the most successful method is also the easiest. Get distracted. Make the decision to literally transform your thoughts into something different, ideally thoughts that are engaging, enjoyable, thrilling, or positive. Instead, when a circumstance calls for loud reflection, many people locate a stop sign and mentally yell the word "stop!"

2. Put yourself out there for excellence. Gain the ability to laugh at difficulties and mistakes, to accept human error, and to see the humour in it as it occurs. Assume that everyone is busy and that there are likely other reasons

for what would otherwise be interpreted as a slight or a power move. Recognize that most of the time, it's not about you.

3. Eliminate causes. Avoid, limit, and think twice as much as you can around individuals or situations that make you feel down. Determine who, what, and how you can lessen your sensitivity to these stimuli.

4. Select "stream." Find activities that you enjoy, whether it be reading, strolling, kayaking, playing the piano, or shooting hoops. Plan the dates and timings of activities in your life on a weekly, or even daily, basis.

5. Study hard, then practise even harder! Finally, choose a few of these advice, instruction, and practise. According to research, it takes a lot of practise to "hardwire" a new habit, so be patience with yourself and keep using your individual overthinking tactics. With time and practise, you ought to become both happier and more effective.

How to Deal with Stress and Anxiety

People who exhibit generalised anxiety frequently have high levels of reactivity, so you can try a relaxing technique like progressive muscle relaxation.

Take up brief, fascinating, entertaining hobbies to occupy your time and divert your attention from persistent negative thoughts. These can be things that have served a purpose in the past. Exercise is a key strategy for reducing anxiety. Exercise causes the release of brain chemicals that combat depression, anxiety, and worry. Exercise also eases anxiety and serves as a distraction from problems. Cardio workouts should be done at least three days a week for a minimum of 30 minutes each time you work out.

Utilize systematic problem-solving techniques to deal with the stressors that cause your worry. Most people frequently lack the necessary coping skills and knowledge to deal effectively with unpleasant situations or life problems, which makes them feel powerless to change their circumstances. These emotions make people anxious.

Everyone faces difficulties and obstacles in life, but if you are always anxious, your issues will be more apparent and difficult to manage. Getting organised problem-solving training can be a good way to combat this. Effective problem-solving strategies decrease, manage, and even eliminate worry in our daily lives.

By facing your worries and tackling them directly but gradually, you can avoid circumstances and behaviours that promote anxiety. You may, for instance, arrange them according to the step you are most afraid of. These fears could be:

- Getting to a meeting late
- avoiding using your phone for an hour
- not using a shopping list when supermarket shopping
- Organizing a birthday celebration
- accepting a request without consulting your calendar
- leaving the house without your phone for the day

Make use of cognitive interventions

People with GAD frequently commit the following two mistakes:

They overestimate the likelihood of disaster because they are constantly on edge. They may think, "This will be a disaster!" or "I had better get ready for the worst case situation," for instance.

They frequently underestimate their capacity to deal with their challenges. They might have ideas such, "I'll have a breakdown," or "I won't be able to handle this circumstance," for example.

What can you do if you struggle with thoughts like these? Simple! Learn to identify upsetting ideas and determine whether they are realistic in order to combat these negative thoughts.

You might need to ask yourself, for instance, what proof you have for these ideas. You might not need to think about it too much if you can't find any. Determining the likelihood that your future concerns will come true may also be the best course of action.

The preconceptions and presumptions that people with GAD have about themselves should also be regularly questioned. For instance, a person may worry that they will never be prepared on time, which may be followed by the notion that they should be held responsible if something goes wrong and the growing conviction that they failed. Although some people think that worrying will stop bad things from happening, this is false. Instead, it makes them more anxious.

The next course of action is to divert attention from the negative ideas once a person has learned to recognise and challenge those thoughts. By identifying and addressing these presumptions, cognitive behavioural therapy helps people come up with healthier and more beneficial beliefs for their own well-being. Interventions based on mindfulness have been found to help you maintain attention.

Adopt Emotion Regulation and Mindfulness

According to recent research, concern may manifest itself as a means of avoiding emotional processing.

Engage in so-called emotion-regulation techniques and mindfulness exercises because they will improve the way you recognise and experience underlying emotions.

Stop taking any drugs that make you sleepy. Don't use binge eating to calm your anxiousness. Although they might temporarily reduce anxiety, it will eventually return. If symptoms persist for more than three months despite taking the aforementioned steps, schedule a time to see a specialist or get CBT instead.

Realistic Strategies for Dealing with Anxiety and Excessive Worrying Symptoms

It's beneficial to get knowledge of strategies we might employ to combat anxiety and excessive concern. Ask yourself these basic yet useful questions if you find yourself in a bad position.

- Is my concern justified?
- Will what I worry about actually occur?
- How can I be certain that my fears will come true?
- Could my scenario have any other conceivable explanation or result?
- Am I attempting to foresee events that will take place in the distant future and over which I have no control?
- Will the worst-case scenario actually happen, and will it be as horrible as I believe it will be?

- Is it important to worry about?
- What would other people think of my concern?

What Impact Does Your Way of Thinking Have?

What will happen if you continue to think the way you are thinking right now? Do you feel motivated to address the issue at hand as a result of thinking about it, or do you feel demoralised and less confident in your ability to do so? Are there circumstances in which your concerns are justified? Yes! We occasionally worry about things that are probable. You will need to confront your worry in this scenario and, if you can, take action.

In that case, you might have to let it go. This can seem unattainable to people who are specialists at worrying. You may, however, tell yourself that there is nothing that could be done to change this at the moment. Then you can find anything else to do to keep your mind occupied and divert your attention from this issue, which is beyond your control.

Is There Really a Problem to Be Fixed?

If there is a problem to be solved, you might need to concentrate on finding a workable solution. In this situation, you can use your problem-solving abilities to confront the issues that are upsetting you.

You can use the following six methodical problem-solving approaches to do this:

- Clearly state what you believe to be the core issue in writing.
- Write down every potential answer you can come up with; don't rule out the terrible ones just yet.
- Think rationally and carefully about each response.
- Decide on the best course of action.
- Consider your approach to working on the solution carefully.
- Do it.

Note: Your anxiety is not your fault. Stressors from daily living can impact a person's thoughts, feelings, and regular functioning.

Anger Management

Anger, like all other fundamental emotions, is intended to make a certain point to us. Our message can be that something has happened or that someone has done something we don't like. The message is missed, though, if our initial reaction to being angry is to lash out or grow furious. Because of this, controlling anger requires mental clarity and composure. You can take a step back and consider your anger rationally while you're calm, which enables you to do so. Additionally, it enables you to accept and affirm your emotions without allowing them to rule your actions.

However, it might be challenging to remain composed when irritated. When something happens that makes us angry, it takes a lot of skill, patience, and maturity to not act out of character. It is considerably simpler to get retribution if someone has offended you. When we believe that others have wronged us, we may get a certain amount of pleasure from seeing them suffer. However, since they don't address the true problems and root of our rage, these remedies are illusory in reality. In the long term, they may even be more harmful to us and our relationships. In light of this, we must learn healthy techniques for managing our anger, even when we believe it is warranted.

What exactly does anger management entail? Basically, anger management is the process of recognising when you are starting to feel angry or upset and then taking the appropriate actions to calm down so that you can deal with your anger more effectively. Many people believe that the goal of anger management is to prevent you from feeling furious. Others even believe it's intended to help people control their emotions. Both of them exhibit a poor comprehension of the function of anger management. Anger is a human emotion that all living things experience at some point in their lives, as we learned previously. Additionally, we already established why trying to control anger over time by stifling it is unsuccessful.

The goal of anger management is to improve your ability to recognise the warning signals of frustration and provide you the tools you need to regulate your anger. Numerous books have been written about anger and how to manage it better. Therefore, reading books like this one might teach one the necessary techniques for handling frustration. However, taking an anger management class or receiving counselling is the most typical way that people learn how to control their anger.

You will learn how to recognise the signals of impending frustration and how to control your emotions so that you may confront your rage with confidence.

Right now, you might be asking yourself, "How can I know if I need anger management classes?" Here are a few indications that you might need to take anger management lessons in order to regulate your rage.

You frequently feel as though you must control your anger

While acting out in fits of rage is not the proper answer to anger, keeping your anger hidden is also not a productive method to deal with it. If you feel like you have to hold your anger within all the time, you may not have the right coping mechanisms. You can also be terrified of being open and honest with others about how you really feel.

Being vulnerable is crucial in any relationship because it fosters mutual trust. Being closed off to one's emotions frequently results in alienation, anxiety, and mistrust. These can lead to increased sentiments of rage and irritation. They are also weak foundations upon which to establish a relationship. Therefore, it's crucial to take responsibility for learning the appropriate coping mechanisms rather than trying to suppress your anger.

You primarily think on unpleasant experiences

True, there are many difficulties in life, and everyone eventually encounters adversity. However, it's crucial to avoid letting the negative things that occur in our life sap our energy and joy. You become diverted from genuinely enjoying your life to the maximum potential if you persistently concentrate exclusively on the negative experiences in it. A nice roof over your head and the company of loved ones are two other basic comforts that you might find it much harder to enjoy. Therefore, in order to keep your anger from becoming habitual, you must develop the appropriate coping mechanisms.

You Constantly Struggle with Feelings of Hostility and Irritation

You must develop anger management techniques if you battle with unsettling feelings of annoyance and animosity toward other people all the time. Even though there are days when life is not ideal, there are still a lot of positive aspects to consider. If your life's circumstances consistently make you angry, you may have underlying anger issues that need to be addressed as soon as possible.

You frequently engage in arguments that make you even angrier.

There are numerous times in life when you will have cause to be genuinely upset with someone. However, if you frequently engage in heated arguments with other people, this may indicate that you have an underlying anger issue. It can also just be an indication that your anger management techniques are ineffective. Perhaps blaming the other person or having a temper tantrum is your first reaction when you're furious. Perhaps you even start having confrontational conversations with the targets of your annoyance. All of these methods for controlling your anger are completely incorrect because they merely make you feel more irritated. Instead, you should learn to de-stress so that you can approach the situation with objectivity.

When you're angry, you act physically violently

Although rage is a perfectly acceptable emotion that can lead to sentiments of hostility, it is never appropriate to express anger through violence. In reality, retaliating physically when you're upset can be highly bad for your relationships, reputation, and health. Additionally, it may result in very significant legal repercussions like being sued or incarcerated for abuse. If you notice that you often act violently when you're furious, you should get help right away. You can interrupt this cycle of bad anger management and learn to express your displeasure in more healthy ways that do not entail using violence by seeking counselling and enrolling in anger management classes.

You act erratically when you're angry.

Perhaps when you're furious, you don't act violently toward others. However, you might have a propensity to shatter or smash objects when you're upset. Even now, using this as a coping mechanism for irritation and rage is inappropriate. This kind of behaviour merely serves to propagate the notion that acting aggressively will make the anger go away by omitting to address the true source of the rage. The fact is that it is ineffective. Finding the source of your anger and using it for good are the only methods to effectively manage it.

You stay away from some situations out of fear of getting angry

Your tendency to avoid situations that can make you angry is another indication that you need anger management training. Perhaps you don't enjoy attending events with your spouse since they frequently leave you alone to mingle with other guests. Another possibility is that you avoid talking to a close friend because you think they are too critical.

Whichever the case, it might be difficult to resist the want to steer clear of any situation that might make you angry. However, avoiding some circumstances out of concern for becoming irritated is not a productive method of controlling your anger. It weakens your ability to take responsibility for your feelings because it transfers the burden of accountability on the other person. Additionally, it merely masks repressed anger that simmers subtly without your knowledge. This could eventually explode in ways that are highly harmful to you and your relationships.

The goal of anger management programmes is primarily to teach students how to recognise when they are becoming angry and take the proper action to deal with the emotion. The programmes are typically held in the form of one-on-one or group sessions with a counsellor or therapist. The length of the anger management programme will vary depending on your needs; it could be a few days, a few weeks, or even a few months. You must therefore exercise patience and view the entire procedure as a learning opportunity.

You will first learn how to recognise stresses and anger triggers when you start taking anger management programmes. You can start to understand the origins of anger and learn how to regulate it by recognising its early warning signs. Stressors are often items in your life that make you angry and aggravate pent-up aggravation. These could be issues with a misbehaving child, money issues, or coworkers who are always talking negatively about you.

Rage management classes will also educate you how to recognise the signs of anger in addition to teaching you how to recognise the triggers. As we have learned, different people experience rage in different ways physiologically. As a result, you might not experience anger in the same way that someone else does. One person's anger may make them sweat and their heart race, while another person's upsetness may make them feel like they have a knot in their stomach. You can recognise the physical signs of anger as they appear specifically in your body by taking anger management classes.

Beginner's anger management is also designed to assist you in identifying the warning signals of rising anger. You can feel the need to be quiet in order to prevent a heated argument or the urge to yell at the person you believe to be the target of your rage. Being conscious of your bodily responses will enable you to take a step back and thoughtfully consider your anger before moving on with the proper answer.

Getting Unstuck from The Past

It's hard to get rid of the ghost of the past. The more forcefully we push it, the louder it becomes. At the most awkward times, it returns to haunt. It shouldn't come as a surprise that you consistently recall all negative events in your life. Your mind makes an excellent storage facility. It can store an infinite amount of data. More than 2.5 petabytes of data can be stored in your brain, according to scientists, and there is still room for more. In reality, it equates to 300 million hours of video storage. It's a big deal.

It indicates that all of the events in your life, both good and bad, are stored in your memory. Your mind, however, also reacts strongly to unpleasant things because it feels the need to replay them over and over to prevent you from encountering the same type of situation. It is a defence system with noble intentions.

When your mind begins incessantly replaying the bad events, it becomes difficult for you to start over. It makes starting over difficult. Your mental clutter plays a significant part in this. You've allowed your history to weigh you down. Some of the compelling causes include fragility, the consolation of victimhood, and the desperate want to stay safe. These emotions invade your time for work. They do not allow for optimistic thinking.

All of this occurs because you are not paying attention. You seek a secure haven because you have let your thoughts to be overtaken by unpleasant memories.

Consider a brief incident. There was once a farmer. He owned a sizable farm, but his previous harvests had been unlucky. Droughts can occasionally impair the harvests, and pest infestations can also ruin them. The farmer came to the conclusion that enough was enough. His harvests were being wrecked anyway, so he wouldn't put up with this nonsense any longer. So he made the safe choice to do nothing and plant nothing. Was that a remedy? Without a doubt, it wasn't a solution. The farmer had previously feared that rain or bugs might harm his harvest. There was a chance he wouldn't obtain the entire crop. But in light of his behaviour, it is certain that he will receive nothing at all. Safe play isn't always the best course of action. This is what the burden of the past does to you.

You will rot in a corner without ever seeing the light of day if you let your mind and thoughts govern your existence. It won't stop reminding you that there are many risks and dangers in the world.

The only way to succeed in this world is to learn from your past mistakes and move on. Your ability to study and succeed will never be possible if your head is filled with anxieties. It won't have the necessary potential. A cluttered mind is unable to distinguish between a safe decision and a decision out of fear.

Safe choices are grounded on facts. They are based on the potential effects of choices and enact corrective measures. The farmer has the option of making different irrigation plans. He may have used pest management techniques. Even if he hadn't done any of these, there was a 50/50 chance of getting a crop. But he decided to do nothing out of dread. The end result was a promise of never having anything. Your insecurities are the source of your fearful choices, and they keep getting stronger. If you do not learn how to combat them, they will subjugate you and render you incapable of appreciating this existence.

How to Stop Thinking Negatively

Humans are superior to other species coexisting on this planet because of our capacity for thought. If you pay close attention, they perform all of our actions. Like humans, they are born, eat, grow, reproduce, and eventually pass away. In essence, there is no distinction between ourselves and other creatures. The only difference between us and other people is our capacity for thought.

However, when our brain starts engaging in negative thinking, this benefit quickly becomes a curse. You are not alone if you believe that the majority of your thoughts are negative, sad, and destructive of yourself. The majority of the human species is troubled by this malice. However, negative thinking has evolved slowly over millions of years as part of mankind's survival strategy.

In this universe, humanity hasn't always been in a favourable position. We were defenceless and exposed. We lacked any weather protection. We lacked the means to organise food and were essentially helpless in the face of the monsters. We could have been killed at any moment due to carelessness. Our minds evolved a negative thought process so they could create a safe outcome by running through all the worst-case situations. It serves more as a defence mechanism.

The situation wouldn't end there if a member of the clan was slain by a beast. In order to develop a plan to prevent a similar outcome in the future, our minds would continually replay the experience. The mind reenacted the identical event and induced dread to prevent us from making the same error. It contributed to our survival. Having negative thoughts has served as our defence mechanism against all dangers for thousands of years.

It is not unfounded if you are thinking negatively about anything comparable right now. Its origins can be found in the same urge for survival that helped you live through the most difficult circumstances. There is a point at which anything turns toxic, though. In order to keep you from acting, your brain will continue to replay frightening scenarios if you give it free rein. Your subconscious is aware that staying inside the shell is your best chance of surviving. The powers of the outside world are uncontrollable and unexpected. It's risky, though, to let this mindset rule you.

Your mind starts to form negative thought patterns as a natural reaction to particular circumstances. Your impression of threat determines how negative your thoughts are. Most of the time, there is absolutely no threat. When you're simply too afraid to do something, your mind starts projecting the worst-case scenarios onto the situation. Inaction, procrastination, worry, and anxiety are the results of this. You are doomed to failure if you fall into this trap. Nothing will happen if you do nothing. Before the vulnerable days, we had come a long way. The day of the savages is behind us. This is a world that is made up of conversations, laws, and structures. The results of activities are calculated. There is a limit to the harm that can be done, even if all hell breaks loose. If you don't take action, the harm has already been done.

Mind clutter includes persistently unfavourable thought patterns that emerge in your brain. Too much negativity is present in your thoughts, and this is reflected in the way you think. If left uncontrolled, this might be dangerous. You might become unsure, terrified, and weak as a result. You can never develop that competitive edge within yourself. You will lose the ability to take risks and develop a scared decision-making style, which will cause you to make no decisions at all. To begin with, this is a pitiful situation. You'll have no longer have any control over your life. Your life's path will first be determined by your imagination and past events. Your personal and professional life, health, family, relationships, job, and more will all suffer as a result.

Understand your negative thought patterns.

As was previously stated, having negative ideas is not a problem; the issue is not being aware of your negative thought patterns. Everyone experiences bad ideas. The only person who is free from dread and bad thoughts is a toddler or a lunatic. Fear has no real significance to them because they are free of it. Since you are a rational person with experience, your mind will naturally entertain unfavourable ideas about objects, people, and events. The key is to continue to be aware of your negative ideas. Negative ideas will intensify if you continue to ignore them. You will be terrified by the repeated playing of even a minor error.

Whether we are awake or asleep, we all occasionally have bad thoughts. Your mind is constantly running the scenario through. It's your responsibility to mentally simulate the situation and apply logic. Once a day, if you do that, you can relax your subconscious. You could have allayed everyone's worries.

Start carefully examining your negative ideas every day if you have negative thought patterns and your fear is impairing your judgement. Spend a set amount of time each day thinking about the current problems and the best course of action. This will make your negative thought patterns easier to manage and enable you to work productively.

You can only make cheese out of spilled milk.

Negativity cannot be eliminated by more negativity. Brooding over an issue won't solve it if one exists. Consider how you can overcome it.

We encounter a number of events every day that are out of our control. Lamenting over them won't advance our cause. The only way to handle such circumstances is to come up with strategies to minimise their impact. If you are running late for work, consider taking a fast route or coming up with a stronger justification. It won't do any good to wallow in your tardiness.

In real life, negative thinking has a similar effect. Instead of dwelling too much on the consequences if you are thinking negatively, consider how you can handle the circumstance. Start thinking about the nice things you want and making a list of the ones you can make happen if a negative thought pattern has started and is bringing all the terrible things to the forefront. You must make due with what you have because positive is the only way to overcome negativity. Consider ways to improve it.

Never again punish yourself

Worrying thoughts are torture. Stress and worry are caused by them. It is generally recognised that stress and worry have a negative effect on both your physical and mental health. They serve as catalysts for the start of various detrimental processes. Your body begins to release stress hormones, which cause fat storage, sluggishness, heartburn, muscle stiffness, and the whole nine yards. These triggers cause your body to behave adversely.

Your anxiety will increase if you make an effort to block out these ideas since your mind will be aware that you are doing so. To deal with such negative thoughts, you need use a 3-step strategy.

Vent: Let these thoughts out. Do not be afraid to consider them. Let them be heard clearly. It will aid you in fully comprehending how bad your thoughts have become. Don't, however, let yourself become sucked into them. Simply consider them, then put them to rest.

Cap: It will be simpler for you to comprehend the breadth of the negative ideas once you have acknowledged their complete scope. They won't be as frightening. You have the opportunity to put an end to them now. Create strategies to combat these unfavourable ideas.

Plan a course of action: You know the size of the issue, you comprehend it, and all you need now is a plan of action to solve it. At this point, you can seek assistance from a variety of sources. Consider your options for resolving the issue. Your relatives and friends can assist you in solving the situation. Online resources for finding solutions are available. The potential solutions are available for reading. It will broaden your viewpoint.

If you continue to punish yourself with negative ideas, they will only get worse. Do not subject yourself to that.

Approach the issue in a systematic way. You can think more clearly if you get rid of the mental clutter.

Put them on paper.

It's a good idea to write down your unfavourable thoughts in order to organise your thinking. The more you think negatively, the more powerful your thoughts will become. The same situations will continue to occur repeatedly.

Negative thoughts can be banished from your head by writing them down. It will assist you in organising your thoughts. Your mind is more capable of thought when one thing is less likely to blend with another. Writing down your thoughts on paper is the best method for clearing the mind.

Positive Attitude Activated

An intense emotion, negativity. It dominates your brain process and manifests itself in a very obvious way. Adopting positivism is the best response to negativity. There may be a dozen terrible things going on in your life right now, but that doesn't mean there isn't positive energy as well. You'll need to constantly remind yourself of the good things going on in the world. This will aid in battling your unfavourable feelings. You need to keep reminding yourself of all the good things in life. Consider the good things that lie ahead. The things you cherish or that make you happy. Break away from your bad habits. Enjoy a few lighthearted moments. Your brain will be relieved of the negative ideas as a result. The negative thought patterns will be simple for you to break.

The adverse mental process is really overwhelming. It has a profound effect on your mental state. You cannot just try to avoid this state. You'll have to work hard to make the situations more enjoyable. The good things in your environment are highly beneficial to the process. Declutter the area around you. Organize your environment to prevent negativity from spreading. Keep your little victories in mind. You will be able to overcome negative thought patterns by taking these small measures to embrace optimism.

Examine the Positive Effects of Negative Thought Patterns

Negative ideas are frequently quite imposing. They remove all other thoughts from our minds. They cause terror. We never pay attention to that degree because we are so afraid. Fear has a powerful hold. It maintains our interest. It has our complete focus. The majority of the time, though, we are so consumed by the anxiety that we exaggerate its power. Consider the merit of any negative thinking patterns or feelings of anxiety that may be arising. If you want to make sure it can inflict the damage you anticipate, look closely.

The purpose of negative thoughts is to warn you. There is no justification for inactivity. Consider whether a worrying notion qualifies to put you in risk if it makes you feel frightened. The majority of the time, nothing serious is happening. It is readily overcomeable. A risk to benefit ratio always exists. Determine the risks and allay your concerns. Negative thought patterns should not be taken at face value. Consider the advantages of your activities and assess whether they outweigh the hazards. Your mental clarity will improve. Negative ideas will not advance your cause if you continue to think about them.

Avoid Receiving Too Much Negative Information

We are in the era of nonstop news coverage. The news is typically not good since it sells quickly and resonates strongly. It is fascinating, and you want to learn more. The main cause of the majority of bad news stories is this. Negativity is pervasive across social media platforms and the internet as a whole. The explanation is straightforward: bad news has a bigger impact than good news. Curiosity is sparked, which prompts more TV viewing, online searches, intrigue, and eventually more sales. But ultimately, this negativity finds its way to you. It makes your day off to a horrible start. One piece of bad news can make you think negatively. You might begin to consider all the issues in your life and connect them to the news.

You live in a time where information is readily available. Never start your day with the news. If necessary, focus just on the news that interests you.

Positive Thinking

Though it sounds simple, it can be difficult to replace negative thoughts with good ones. Actually, the majority of individuals don't really grasp the concept of negative thinking. Happiness may depend on how one manages these unpleasant thoughts rather than on a few negative thoughts.

It's crucial to make an effort to keep one's optimism despite any setbacks and difficulties. Contrary to popular belief, there are more advantages to avoiding negative thinking. Actually, positive psychology is slowly but surely receiving more attention within the discipline of psychology. It entails the investigation of the physiological and psychological impacts of constructive attitudes, actions, and routines.

According to research, those who think positively generally find life to be more enjoyable. Actually, optimistic people are miles ahead of the competition in terms of their physical, mental, and stress levels. Positive thinking is helpful for healing, but people must realise they must not believe the lies their minds are telling them.

Additionally, they ought to strive to identify the source of their negative beliefs. The first thing to keep in mind is that negative thoughts are the result of false presumptions and convictions. Therefore, dismissing these ideas is insufficient. Everyone deserves to be loved and happy, and people should never forget this.

Among the causes to quit thinking negatively are:

Ability to Cope with Stress

Stressful situations, such losing a job or having a domestic argument, are common for people. The way people respond to difficult circumstances makes all the difference. However, studies show that those with a more upbeat view frequently take a more optimistic response to challenging circumstances.

People that think positively take the contrary approach rather than waste time on unchangeable negative ideas about things gone wrong. They come to terms with the fact that they cannot change some circumstances and discover more effective coping mechanisms.

Better Mental Health

One who thinks more optimistically is less likely to struggle with issues like sadness and anxiety. Experts claim that optimists have a higher quality of life than pessimists, including better psychological health.

Contrary to popular assumption, positive thinking has the ability to treat specific mental disorders and habits.

There is no reason to worry for those who do not consider themselves. It's possible to break negative thought habits and begin to reap the rewards of positive thinking. For instance, being still is an excellent method to combat negativity. Through meditation, people can learn to disengage from their unfavourable ideas.

Better Physical Health

Some individuals think that persons who think positively are the only ones who can practise good behaviours, like exercising frequently. This isn't always the case, though. Even those who experience frequent negative thoughts can learn to concentrate on their physical health by improving their diet and engaging in regular exercise, even if they typically have a stronger drive to do so.

Another idea holds that persons who are optimistic have better physical health because they can handle stress better or perhaps because they experience less stress. As a result, stress has much less of a detrimental impact on their physical health. For the following health advantages, it is crucial to quit worrying about one's negative thoughts:

- a longer life
- reduce the risk of cardiovascular disease

- quicker recovery from ailments and injuries
- Boost your immune system's power
- improved general wellbeing

Why You Shouldn't Be Alarmed by Your Negative Thoughts

People frequently think that negative ideas are harmful or even toxic, which is why so many people worry about them. Negative ideas, in the opinion of some "experts," diminish people's positive vibes, keep them focused on negativity, and so forth. In essence, they instruct individuals on how to rid themselves of negative thoughts in order to feel confident and secure.

Getting rid of negative ideas is supposedly linked to professional success, a higher vibration, inner peace, better boyfriends/girlfriends, and many other benefits, according to several web articles and self-help books. People who have negative ideas flowing through their brains all the time often wonder what to deal with them.

They ponder how to stop such ideas from occurring or whether it is indeed possible to compel a positive thought to take precedence over a bad one. Unfortunately, because they do not grasp what thoughts, both good and negative, are in the first place, most individuals have a tendency to misunderstand the entire subject of negative thinking.

People's happiness is not determined by their bad ideas; rather, it is determined by what they do with those thoughts. The good news is that because of the following, people do not need to worry as much about their negative thoughts:

Having some unfavourable ideas is common.

Every day, the human mind processes many thoughts, the most of which are unfavourable. In fact, conversing with and meeting a person who never thinks negatively would be interesting. Even those who constantly seem positive carry a lot of bad baggage in their brains.

For instance, a person who is walking around bragging about their new car may actually be trying to mask unfavourable feelings and promote the notion that they weren't good enough before purchasing the vehicle. In essence, people shouldn't worry about having negative ideas in the first place since experiencing them is a natural aspect of being human.

Negative beliefs are not always founded in reality

Negative thoughts do not have to be believed by individuals. Not all thoughts are true, despite what the mind would have you believe. Because a person's intellect is only a small portion of who they are, it is crucial to keep one's thoughts and sense of self distinct. The four parts of a human being are actually:

a) Physical body

b) Mind

c) Spiritual aspect

d) Heart

As a result, the human mind is simply a very useful tool, and each person's particular set of beliefs serves as a filter for their perceptions and thoughts. This filter produces negative thoughts because negativity exists within the filter. As a result, when people make an effort to heal and develop, what they are truly doing is altering their lenses or paradigms.

People shouldn't examine or worry about their negative ideas because everyone is perfect in their own unique manner. The only way to get rid of them is to stop listening to them because they are just thoughts. One will feel satisfied and at peace when their mind is at rest. When one chooses not to accept their negative thoughts, this is doable.

It is possible to change one's negative thoughts into positive ones.

There is nothing wrong with choosing optimism, but as was mentioned above, it's crucial to keep in mind that because negative thoughts are frequently false, they don't actually matter in the first place. Furthermore, they don't turn a person into a horrible person or a less-than-human creature.

People who automatically strive to confront and reject their bad ideas are subconsciously reminding themselves that they are unworthy. They basically said that good people shouldn't think bad thoughts. However, this belief is equally as unfavourable as their initial impressions.

The seemingly insignificant action of recognising the unfavourable thinking and choosing not to accept it is crucial for personal development. Fortunately, doing this consistently will make it simpler to spot negative thoughts when they arise and will lead to fewer of them.

Therefore, adopting a positive outlook is not the only path to recovery; rather, the quickest path to recovery and development is realising that one's poor feelings are a result of entertaining and buying into negative notions. Finding the source of one's negative thoughts might also be useful. It could be simpler to dismiss them, though, given the majority of them are based on false assumptions.

Is Stressing Negative Thought?

An example of negative thinking is worrying. It is common for thoughts to have significant effects. People tend to encounter pleasant things when they think and act positively. On the other hand, those who entertain and believe their negative beliefs frequently experience unfavourable outcomes. Excessive concern reinforces unfavourable attitudes and thoughts in people.

People tend to dwell on and worry about negative thoughts, which unfortunately often come true. People's worries and thoughts have a significant impact on their life. People unintentionally encourage a certain thing to become a reality by worrying about it all the time.

People can start to address and alter their negative ideas once they are aware of the connection between worrying and negative thinking. As a result, people will start to pay attention to things, which will have a favourable impact on their lives.

Identify Your Core Values

The convictions and beliefs that serve as a person's compass in daily life are referred to as core values. As they pursue what is proper and what society expects of them, people make a conscious decision to engage in these actions.

The following describe core values: they can be specific, they can vary from culture to culture, they can cause discord between individuals, they can be learned early in life through family or friends, and they are frequently emotive.

There are various kinds of core values. Family, moral, social, sociocultural, material, spiritual, environmental, intellectual, financial, and self-care values are a few of the categories.

Respect, honesty, freedom, fearlessness, dignity, loyalty, trust, cooperation, care for others, initiative, justice, peace, humour, generosity, adventure, friendships, and excellence are a few examples of core values that spring from the aforementioned categorization.

Because they represent people's wants, desires, and the things they care about most in life, core values are important. Core values are remarkably effective at bringing people's identities together. In addition to providing decision-making principles, core values aid in a person's connection to their true selves.

Motives For Creating Personal Core Values

Core values are important variables that influence an individual's development. The principles encourage people to pursue their personal goals and live happier lives.

The reasons why it's so important for people to establish their own fundamental beliefs are as follows.

Self-awareness is promoted through core principles.

People can learn about their strengths and limitations by using their core values. This is due to the fact that being honest with oneself about one's identity is the first step in developing self-awareness.

Being honest with oneself is made possible by the value of honesty. People can better understand their strengths and weaknesses in this way. Sincere people don't make an effort to appear better than they actually are.

People can better comprehend themselves and accept what they cannot alter by using wisdom. Realizing that they can't expect success if they don't know how to apply their skills also helps people.

A basic attribute of humility is the ability to appreciate what other people are doing. A humble individual lets other people enjoy their accomplishments and enjoy the spotlight. A modest individual will not put themselves first at the expense of others.

Core values aid in self-discovery so that individuals can lead fulfilling lives.

Core values provide guidance.

Core values serve as a guide for behaviour. Standards that define one's identity and what one holds in high regard are considered to be one's core values. Despite the fact that people sometimes fall short of these expectations, the values serve as a guide for their behaviour.

Employers manage firms unethically in the professional sphere. These unethical actions include making false claims regarding a product's efficacy or having mission statements that do not correspond to the actions of the business.

Those who live by their ideals do not act in ways that are deemed acceptable by others. He or she has the option to leave a position where it would be necessary to sacrifice their morals. By doing this, the person stops blindly adhering to social norms and instead lets his or her principles guide their behaviour.

People can use their core values to determine whether their actions are in line with what they deem to be important.

Integral principles guide behaviour

People's thoughts, feelings, words, and eventually actions are influenced by their core beliefs. The values of a person provide context for their behaviour. An honest individual makes an effort to be honest. A person who appreciates transparency will therefore make an effort to be transparent at all times.

When it comes to material items, a person who values their family dedicates their time to spending it with them and supports family ties. Similar to this, someone who places a high value on fitness is more likely to adopt daily routines and lifelong behaviours that support fitness.

A person can behave in ways that are consistent with their principles in the workplace. People hold diverse ideals, hence conflict might happen at work. However, businesses work to teach universal fundamental principles that will act as a behavioural compass for everyone.

For instance, a business may not have any control over the factors that influence how various people's values and behaviour. However, the business may make an effort to persuade staff members to behave in a way that is acceptable to the business through training initiatives and codes of conduct. Thus, core values have a critical role in dictating and directing conduct.

Core values promote individuality and unravel them.

Core principles let individuals see how wonderful and distinctive each individual is. While some people value safety more than adventure, others do. Additionally, some individuals could desire seclusion while others would value public attention.

A person who cherishes solitude, for instance, can feel oppressed if they allow their friend to persuade them to attend a party. The person might agree to accompany you, but they won't be having fun. People may be the friend's lifeline, providing them with beverages and endless chat.

Because everyone is unique, what makes one person delighted could make another feel distant and anxious. As a result, a person needs to be aware of their ideals and follow them without hesitation.

Because of this, when a person follows their beliefs, they recognise their own uniqueness as well as the uniqueness of others, and they learn to respect and value this in others.

Meaningful talks are based on core principles.

A meaningful conversation occurs when the participants are fully engaged and not sidetracked by their thoughts or the activities of others. A good discussion also involves participants being honest, open, and willing to express their feelings.

A conversation is not likely to be truthful when one party is unwilling to express what he or she believes or feels. Transparency, honesty, openness, and sincerity are values that aid in meaningful communication.

Sensitivity is important in meaningful talks as well. When someone is sensitive, they are aware of others' want to talk about difficult situations, and they actively seek them out to do so. When someone discloses an embarrassing circumstance, the hearing party should remain silent, pay close attention, and, if appropriate, offer some advice. One value that can significantly improve someone's self-esteem is care for others.

One meaningful conversation is all it takes to drastically alter someone else's life.

Core principles aid in developing wisdom in difficult circumstances.

Every aspect of a person's life is influenced by their core principles. Making judgments and communicating with others are examples of how the values are displayed. A person's values are typically shaped by his or her experiences in life and the people closest to them.

When a person cherishes spending time with their spouse but is required to work long hours, internal conflict and stress will result. In such a situation, the individual must return to his or her values in order to seek assistance.

The person's values will aid in understanding their highest priority in life, which will enable them to make the greatest choice for themselves.

Living in accordance with one's ideals is necessary for one to develop into the best version of oneself. As a result, the values will serve as the cornerstone for the individual's objectives and meaning in life.

Your confidence is boosted by your core principles.

When a person is certain of his or her core values, achieving confidence becomes simple. A person feels less comfortable interacting with others when they are unsure of their values.

The ability to create thoughts around one's core ideals is what gives one more confidence. People frequently hold contrasting views on the topic at hand during interactions. Because people's fundamental beliefs influence their ideas and opinions, this is true. Every person's "point of view" typically derives from their set of values. That is what causes bias in discourse and other spheres of life.

As a result, a person's basic values enable them to express an opinion, stand out in a crowd, or engage in stimulating relationships. Uncertain of their ideals makes it impossible for a person to speak their opinion or engage in free-wheeling conversation.

How To Find Your Core Value Using These Tips

How can your essential values be discovered and developed?

Observe yourself and learn

Start by posing the following inquiries to yourself: What two things from my youth were missing? What are the two things that I think about most of the time? What are the two topics that I talk about the most? What are the top two expenses for me? How would I characterise my ideal home?

You will see that you learned at least nine things about yourself after asking and responding to these questions. Given that context, it will be simple for you to identify the memories or objects that you cherish or still hold dear.

Consider the role models you have.

Do you have any role models in your life? You might be admiring a member of your family, a close friend, a teacher from elementary school, a professor from a university, a famous person, a celebrity, or even the staff member at your favourite restaurant.

Next, reflect on why you admire each of them. You might be in awe of the values they uphold. For instance, you can tell that the employee at your favourite restaurant actually enjoys their work when they are serving customers and are usually smiling. You respected your elementary school teacher's exceptional listening skills and charisma because she always listened to every kid with sincerity.

List the particular values that each person on your list embodied. You may be motivated to adopt their values.

Consider your life's most unpleasant experiences.

You were where? Why were you upset? You may find that you cherish inclusion and compassion if you have felt the agony of exclusion by others.

Even though suffering is an unpleasant experience, it teaches people lessons about things they would rather not repeat. They thus form values regarding what they find important. You may have gained tolerance, resiliency, humility, empathy, and independence as a result of your suffering.

Remember your happiest memories from your life.

Who or what were you? What made you delighted about that? Did others experience your joy? They were who? What additional elements played a role in your joy?

Find instances from your time in school, your job, your family, and your personal life as you reflect on those times. You'll learn that every experience is crucial and worthwhile for the lessons it teaches about values.

List your fundamental personal values.

Make a list of your main values first. After then, read through the list and consider the situations in which each value might be applicable.

Consider having to choose between moving to a new country to explore new prospects and staying put because it is a more familiar area while weighing the merits of adventure and security. Work your way through your list of values until you find those that speak to you.

Modify your behaviours and outlook

Confidence, emotional restraint, and breaking psychological patterns are all closely related. In all of the polls, interviews, and studies that have been undertaken over the years, participants and researchers have consistently stated this to be true: confidence is essential for any endeavour one does.

A person's self-esteem and confidence can be affected by a wide range of diverse life situations, with adolescence having the biggest impact on one's self-perception. Humans go through adolescence. Men and women receive the most of their emotional education during this time since it contains the highest inclusion of elements like those listed below for most people:

initial romantic liaisons (often tumultuous with lots of highs and lows) • First deep friendships that are tested by adjusting hormones, changing personalities and other life factors that may arise without warning

- First significant achievements and successes, such as accolades from abroad, college scholarships, and summer internships
- learning to drive and becoming aware of the responsibilities that come with doing so
- developing decision-making abilities that are influenced by how teenagers manage peer pressure, balance school, job, and social lives, and make their first life-changing decisions like whether to continue their education after completing their compulsory education.

How could someone's self-esteem and confidence levels be hampered or even destroyed with all of these amazing developments occurring? Unfortunately, in addition to all the positive things that happen to boys and girls during their adolescence, there are a lot of negative things that also happen to them (in greater quantities and with greater intensity than most people do throughout the rest of their lives), like learning to distinguish between affectionate teasing from friends and family and harmful teasing and bullying that comes from those who mean them harm.

- Physical modifications to their skin, muscles, and other body components that may call for care from over-the-counter medicines or even prescription drugs from healthcare professionals

- The development of skills via experience and education can result in emotional shifts that are frequently unanticipated and out of control.
- There is a lot of dread and confusion since it feels like everything is changing around them without any sense of direction or a turning point.

Though hardly everyone left adolescence with more unpleasant than pleasant memories, for those who did and discover that their adult lives are being negatively impacted by those unpleasant experiences or recollections, never fear! There is always something you can do to boost your confidence and self-esteem in order to increase your general life satisfaction and progress toward your objectives.

Self-Esteem and Confidence Levels: How Do They Relate and Differ?

Self-esteem and confidence are frequently referred to as being synonymous when they are discussed. Although they are frequently linked, self-esteem and confidence are actually two distinct personality traits that can be harmed or impaired on their own and require specialised attention to help them be rebuilt and strengthened.

Pro tip: Before focusing on developing self-esteem and confidence, people should aim to master, or at least become more familiar with, the talent of self-awareness. It is challenging to decide where your concentration should be directed and what types of goals you should set to achieve your ultimate hopes and aspirations without knowing where you stand psychologically, physically, and emotionally.

Exercise in Self-Awareness: Listen to Yourself Talk and Take Notes

Listening to how they are saying to themselves, whether out loud or in their minds, is one of the finest methods for someone to comprehend their emotional state and the reason they are feeling the way they are about anything. Everyone has a small voice in their head that expresses honest opinions about what they are thinking or doing, even if those comments are occasionally discouraging or even harsh. Because these are the only ideas, thoughts, and opinions that pass through a person's mind while they are alone (especially if they are stated vocally) or whenever they have the chance, this voice can be believed to be the person's most honest thinking (for those who play the voice in their minds where only they ever hear them).

Self Talk that furthers undermines one's perception of oneself or opinion of one's talents is frequently repeated in the minds of people who have poor self-esteem and confidence levels. The purpose of this exercise is to make people more conscious of their self-talk and how it sounds so they can adjust their present way of thinking or emotional state whenever their self-talk becomes unpleasant.

When you sense your inner voice turning negative, whether it's due to dissatisfaction with an aspect of your appearance or a poorly constructed sentence in a previous social interaction, it will start to make judgmental remarks or attempt to focus on other delicate or underdeveloped aspects of your personality in an effort to lower your mood even more.

- One of the most detrimental activities a person may engage in is self-deprecation and attacks on one's own position or talents. Often, this voice emerges silently and only expresses anxieties and worries when the brain senses that the individual is emotionally vulnerable.
- Take a step back and centre your thoughts when this habit begins to dominate them. When the Self Talk begins, pay attention to those thoughts and how your inner voice (or vocal tone) sounds.
- How would you describe the tone of your voice or inner voice?
- Is it hurtful, furious, or sad?

- Does it convey any emotion at all, or does it just show a more emotionless aspect of you?
- What language does that voice use?
- Do they offend you?
- Are these words you don't typically use when conversing with others?
- When is this voice the loudest?
- When under stress, does the self talk tend to be more negative or more targeted? Or whenever your mind is free of other thoughts?
- Do you control the voice's level of activity with your own thoughts, deeds, and behaviours? Or does it become more active after speaking with others?

Why This Exercise Is Effective: This practise is effective because it draws on a universal human trait shared by both men and women, an inner voice that is in charge of expressing our innermost, most private thoughts regarding the deeds and words we utter each day. It has been shown to be one of the most useful exercises for enhancing emotional intelligence, self-awareness, and how people perceive their own private thoughts when frequently practised.

Who Benefits the Most from This Exercise For individuals who are committed and determined to take charge of their emotional and psychological health, this exercise has shown to be the most beneficial. When this practise becomes a habit and becomes a part of a person's daily routine, they will see a noticeable improvement in their ability to better understand who they are and what makes them tick in order to improve their interactions with others or say yes to more possibilities.

A person is better able to create an actionable plan for how to first raise their self-esteem and confidence levels before moving on to more steadfast and challenging psychological habits like compulsive overthinking and procrastination once they become comfortable with self-awareness habits and have a better understanding of where their emotional health is at. But what exactly is self-esteem, and why is it so crucial to develop it when it comes to improving emotional intelligence and well-being?

What Is Self-Esteem?

The most typical definition of self-esteem is how one feels about themselves overall. Self-esteem and confidence levels frequently have different emotional connections for different people.

This characteristic encompasses a person's potential feelings toward:

- their present state of life

- their position today
- Their position as a couple
- Their key objectives and how they plan to achieve them
- They are surrounded by friends and family.
- their physical attributes and areas of interest

These are just a few of the several elements and aspects that might influence how someone perceives themselves and how confident they feel in themselves. Everyone would probably notice a lot of essential elements that are repeated if they prepared a list of the qualities and characteristics that they consider when they consider how they see themselves. There will, however, be just as many differences as there are similarities, according to numerous experts and specialists who study the effects of self-esteem on people. This is due to the fact that each person has unique ideals or expectations of oneself based on a wide range of additional circumstances, including:

- the setting in which they were raised
- the ideals taught in them by their families when they were little
- Their individual life experiences have led to the development of their personal views and values.
- The standards they have for themselves, as well as those around them, and the expectations they set

These are only a few of the many elements that can influence a person's development. One will learn more about oneself and develop a higher sense of self-worth as they delve further into their own thoughts, feelings, ideas, hopes, and dreams.

What It Is Made Of: The most frequent factors that influence a person's self-esteem are their emotional contacts and experiences. All of life's experiences—mistakes, victories, mishaps, and successes—bring their own emotional and psychological effects. These factors have the biggest impact on how someone considers themselves, their existing way of life, and other aspects of their circumstances. A person's self-esteem will improve and their emotional stability in challenging situations will increase the more positive influences and experiences they may amass.

What Is Confidence (or Self-Confidence)?

When a person expresses self-confidence, they are referring to their faith in their own knowledge, experience, talents, and abilities. A person's confidence levels will vary depending on how much faith they have in what they know, what they say, and what they do in their interpersonal and professional contacts.

What It Is Made Of: A person's view of and faith in their own skills and abilities are the source of their confidence.

Most frequently, good events like job advancements or academic honours lead to this confidence and faith. Their self-confidence will grow as they get more experience and evidence that they are knowledgeable about what they are doing or talking about, which will have a beneficial impact on other parts of their life.

Many people who have high levels of self-esteem yet struggle with confidence, especially in instances where they don't have time to prepare for the task at hand or when they want to express a question but are worried about how others will respond, so they choose to keep their mouths shut. Alternately, individuals may possess high levels of self-assurance and faith in their own skills, but yet suffer from low levels of self-esteem as a result of experiencing heartbreak in a failed relationship or from trust issues brought on by being betrayed by a friend or coworker.

Why Is It So Important for Men and Women to Develop and Strengthen These Characteristics?

There are many circumstances and events that can be triggered by interrelated levels of self-esteem and confidence, as varied as they may be. The better off a person will be in every opportunities they try or goals they pursue throughout their life, the more understanding, experience, and control they have over their own self-esteem and confidence levels.

A person's total mental, psychological, and emotional health can be improved by strengthening these attributes, but there are many other advantages that can also aid an individual's personal health and wellness in a variety of ways.

The Many Advantages of Self-Esteem and Confidence Development

There are countless reasons to stay motivated and focused on work toward improving one's self-esteem and confidence, even for those who are content with their control over chronic overthinking and procrastination. Here are some of the most well-known and frequently mentioned advantages people have discovered in their pursuits of more self-worth and self-assurance!

People pleasers and the development of people-pleasing habits are less likely to occur in those with higher self-esteem and self-confidence than those with lower assessments of themselves or their talents.

Additionally, they typically receive higher performance evaluations and more success in leadership positions.

In addition to being friendlier with clients or other audiences, they are also better able to uplift morale among coworkers or their employers in times of high demand or heightened stress.

These are more aware of their own mental, psychological, and emotional changes and how they effect their day-to-day performance, which increases their chances of creating and achieving both personal and professional goals.

People who have higher levels of self-esteem and confidence report enjoying their life more on a personal and professional level. They are also more willing to seize opportunities when they are presented.

They also frequently start conversations with people they do not know and are more confident than those who doubt themselves and hesitate around others, making them braver and more dominating in their social circles and work teams.

These are just a few of the advantages that study and research participants of various ages and lifestyles have mentioned during the course of their journeys toward personal betterment! Based on the techniques they choose to use, how committed they can be to their self-improvement plan, and of course, what specific issues and concerns they are trying to improve or eliminate, each person will find a whole new array of benefits and progress markers that are specialised and more tailored to their individual needs.

Form Good Habits

Procrastination is one of the main issues associated with overthinking. In reality, the brain's primary goal while producing worry is to make you inactive. In order to reduce the risk, it urges you to remain in a corner. As we've already mentioned, this is a viable method for surviving in the wild. Living in a society where your contribution matters is not the way to go.

One of the most prevalent negative effects of overthinking is procrastination. It keeps you stuck in an inaction-based, never-ending thought cycle. Your mind is capable of continually creating tactics, dismissing them after a while, and then creating new, improved ones. There is no end to how many times this process can be repeated.

To interrupt the cycle of contemplation and take action, you actually need a strategy. It will get more difficult to avoid overthinking about it the longer you continue to do so. If they are not put into practise, even the best strategies in the world risk failure.

One of the most detrimental characteristics of an overthinker is procrastination, which would also reinforce your practise of delaying taking action.

You can use the five tactics listed below to help you stop thinking and start acting. To end the impasse, choose one of these options based on the circumstances. Remember that it will be more difficult for you to escape the impasse the longer you stay there.

The 5 Second Rule

The association between fear and delaying things is extremely ingrained. The mind naturally begins to overthink something when you are afraid of performing it, the results, or dislike it. It both makes you consider the repercussions if something goes wrong and would also lead you to believe that something will. Many times, if you don't take action right away, your mind will be able to persuade you that the time has passed and that taking the action now is pointless.

The mind enjoys keeping you seated and bound to thoughts. The mind considers that to be the most secure playing field.

Only tasks that we dislike doing are put off until later. the things we don't feel really passionate about or the things that were imposed upon us. We anticipate the things we are passionate about.

Despite the alarm clock going off multiple times and being snoozed, some still find it difficult to get out of bed in the morning. Their lack of enthusiasm for getting up is the cause. They are not energised by the day's possibilities.

The same people would wake up quite early if they had something they were truly enthusiastic about.

You cannot, however, be enthusiastic about everything you need to do. Not at all about the things you despise or dread. However, staying still will simply encourage you to overthink.

Make it a rule to act after having an idea for no more than five seconds. There is hardly any time left. But you are not required to complete the task in five seconds. You only need to start.

For instance, you must get out of bed within five minutes of the alarm clock sounding if you need to travel to the office. Your first preference if you stayed any longer would be to take one last nap.

As soon as you get past the 5-second mark, your mind will begin to overthink the entire procedure and will undoubtedly come up with arguments to support its futility.

Act quickly before it's too late. This is a fantastic method for escaping the chains of procrastination.

Ditching the Autopilot

The majority of the decisions we make are not consciously made. They are the choices made based solely on instinct. We don't actually give them much thought. This occurs since our minds operate primarily in autopilot mode.

If you have not put much pressure on it to make meaningful decisions, it prefers to base decisions on references. what you previously accomplished in comparable circumstances. Did they produce any unfavourable results? What chances do you think the actions in this attempt have of succeeding?

Based on the answers to these questions, your mind's autopilot directs your actions. Never is the situation evaluated on its own merits. The likelihood of success this time and the circumstances that might influence the outcome are not pleasant to the psyche. It desires to remain inert. The majority of people avoid taking action because of procrastination. Without even giving them a passing thought, their minds quickly rule out the majority of the alternatives. You'll spend the remaining time you have right now overthinking.

You must turn off the autopilot if you wish to escape the overthinking trap. Observe the objects with awareness. Make every choice deliberately. Don't try to make too many assumptions; instead, consider each scenario on its own merits. When you stop making many assumptions, this will provide you a better foundation for action and prevent you from overthinking.

Starting Positively

Our propensity to see things negatively is one of the main reasons we hesitate to take any form of action. We expect things to start out poorly and then turn around to be good. Almost seldom does this work.

The initiative suffers from the demoralising negative mindset process. Chiding your own thinking won't motivate you; instead, it'll paralyse you.

Any new endeavour, even a new day, should be begun with good intentions. Don't burden it with expectations because doing so could cause you to worry. Simply begin on a hopeful tone, believing that things will get better from where you are.

Try shifting your perspective if you believe that your limited view prevents you from seeing things positively from that standpoint. Put yourself in the position of the person who you believe would perform the task more competently. Think about it from a new angle. Sometimes, altering one's point of view can completely transform a piece of work. Things that appear really difficult to your angel may be simple to others.

A man once wandered through a village looking for a well-known church. He had travelled a distance on foot and was becoming irritable. He stopped a boy who was in the path and asked him how far the church was. After giving it some thought, the boy responded with 24,858 kilometres. The man was amazed and in shock. The church couldn't be that far away, he claimed. I travelled a great distance in search of it.

According to the boy's route, it was 24,858 miles, but if he had gone the other way, it would have been just 2 miles.

Sometimes we just view things from a really challenging perspective. A different point of view can completely alter the narrative.

It might make the work enjoyable and simple. If you're feeling stuck at work and don't see a way out, try thinking about the situation from the perspective of someone else.

Acknowledging the Fears

Fears have the power to paralyse us. It significantly affects how well we can make decisions. Our anxieties will continue to round us if we don't confront them. Even when we actively avoid our worries, our minds do not remain mute; they constantly force us to consider our anxieties and the effects of our choices.

No way out of this cycle exists. Recognizing your anxieties is the only way to successfully avoid it.

When you accept your concerns, they stop having a lethal effect. You can obviously see what type of an effect they will have. You have the opportunity to see through your worries and clearly determine your possibilities of success.

This is an effective strategy to end the impasse and eliminate the fear-driven procrastination habit.

Developing Your Milestone Setting Skills

Our mind is always trying to find reasons to make us do nothing. It attempts to make you do nothing since that is the most secure course of action.

Many people who started out working ambitiously eventually fail—not because they made inadequate efforts, but rather because their minds were able to persuade them that their efforts were in vain.

For instance, you want to get slender and shed 30 pounds. You may be inspired to start working in that direction by your objectives, outside motives, and sources of inspiration. However, because you will be working against your own body, it is a process that need ongoing motivation. Your work would be difficult because of the body. The body would help the mind with that.

This implies that it may become very challenging to stay motivated after a few days. You won't be able to complete the goal of 30 pounds in a matter of days or weeks, therefore there is a great likelihood that you will give up.

Many people give up even before they start because they begin to overthink the chances of success and discover none.

Imagine your aim now if it had been more precisely defined and divided into smaller milestones.

30 pounds lost in 6 months seems like a much more specific objective. There is a deadline, thus you are not allowed to keep pushing it back. This is the start of your fight against procrastination.

However, 6 months is a very long time, and it can be challenging to stay motivated even with a clear goal.

To aid you in your endeavour, milestones are also necessary.

With the aid of milestones, you can organise your results into more manageable sections and monitor your progress.

You have 24 weeks to drop the 30 pounds you need to lose in order to reach your 6-month weight loss goal. Now we are at 1.25 pounds per week.

Weekly goals can serve as a steady source of motivation for you. There will be weeks when you lose weight more slowly. Your next week's efforts to make up the shortfall would be motivated by the milestones.

There will be weeks when your accomplishments are higher, and the milestones will motivate you to work more to reach the end result more quickly.

You can break the cycles of procrastination and inaction by setting specific goals, breaking them into smaller milestones, and taking fast action.

Make it a habit to keep a diary

A fantastic way to organise your thoughts is to keep a journal. People frequently underrate the value of daily thought-journaling. You can get rid of stuff from your mind that you might not be aware of through journaling. It makes sure that you can successfully manage stress and improves working memory. Similar to this, the practise of writing down your everyday events in a notebook encourages you to express any suppressed feelings. As a result, you make room for life's fresh experiences. This has the result of allowing you to get rid of any nervousness you may have been feeling.

Write Goals, Emotions, Results

It has been referred to in a variety of ways as either the best part of living or our reasons for existing. the thoughts, emotions, or passions we awaken each morning to pursue. Our objective. Maybe it's just a pastime that we enjoy doing a lot. Now is the moment to begin considering how you want to fill that empty space where the disorganised thoughts of your mind formerly took root. However you want to describe it. Time for another another mental workout.

Recall your youth, whether as a child or adolescent. When you were a child, did you have any happy memories? Did you spend most or all of your leisure time honing a particular sport, talent, or hobby? Perhaps you like reading and spent every summer break reading a tonne of books. Did you prefer swimming over anything else? Basketball or baseball games? astride a horse? sketching and drawing? Maybe the anticipation of each day was simply hanging out with friends, laughing, and talking. Whatever it was, if you can, try to recall a moment when you were engaged in a hobby you loved. How did it make you feel? Do you still recall how happy it made you feel?

Many adults hold the false belief that once we reach adulthood, the joy we once felt would never return. This is the furthest thing from the truth. It's not a requirement of life that we give that up once we reach a certain age; each of us still has that child inside of us. Many people have made their early interests into successful and rewarding careers. Every day, they get to recapture the happiness they felt as kids—but this time, they get paid for it!

We don't have to give up the most priceless aspects of being a child as we get older, like mental freedom, fun, curiosity, and passion. It's time to figure out how to bring that joy into your life right now, therefore I want you to think back to the things that brought you joy when you were a kid. I'm not suggesting that you try to go back in time or become a child. I'm trying to convey that it is possible for adults to feel joy and presence in the same way that children do. We are simply being told that there is no room for these things by society and other busy minds. Let's disprove them!

Take out the paper once more, perhaps just turning the sheet you were working on over.

Making a list of the things you enjoyed doing as a child may be useful. Go look for your old home videos, dance performance photos, boy scout group pictures, etc. Spend some time reflecting on the delight that these items brought you.

Now consider your current favourite activities. When was the last time you had sufficient free time to engage in an activity you loved? It could take a little longer to think of what you enjoy doing if it has been a while. Do not lose heart. You can always choose a topic you'd want to research; who knows, it might turn out to be your new interest!

In order to bring enjoyment and relaxation into your life, list a few things you'd like to truly focus on. You may have a tonne of things you like to do, but you should avoid getting too busy. Let's pick one or two things that you would like to start incorporating into your life since the majority of people won't be able to quit their jobs and pursue all of their loves full-time (wouldn't that be the life!).

When I say "create some time to commit to your joy," I mean that you should strive and prioritise doing something simply for you every day. The last thing you want to do is turn your pastime become a chore. Maybe all that has to be done is to take a nap! Making time for yourself is a fantastic approach to combine with the interruption strategy we previously discussed to completely change the way your brain processes your daily life. You are likely familiar with this phenomenon if you experience the same inner dread each morning upon realising that you must get out of bed and travel to work each day. Even though it may seem unattainable right now, I guarantee that by the end of this book, you will have learned the crucial measures to take in order to realise a happy and fulfilling everyday life.

Consider locating and enrolling in a class that is connected to something you've always wanted to learn or try if, like me, you need structure. Find a class, perhaps a free community class in your city, if you used to love drawing but it's been a while. You might meet some people who share your interests! You'll discover that the more you strive for personal improvement, the more it will come to you naturally. After practising mind awareness, you'll inevitably start to see things that were previously invisible to you because there were too many competing thoughts.

Chapter 3: Tips for Cleaning Up Your Environment

Code name: Minimalism

Principles of a Minimalist Approach

1. Less is more.

Aristotle discussed how most of our interactions are based on utility and convenience and are devoid of any real meaning in his Nicomachean Ethics. However, when we hold on to just one or two meaningful connections, we prioritise the ones that improve our general wellbeing. You'll enjoy life far more if you can concentrate on a small number of truly satisfying connections because you'll be less concerned with what other people think of you and more concerned with how you may lead a happier life.

2. End unhealthy connections.

The second thing you need to do is end any toxic relationships that are negatively influencing your life. When someone drains all the energy out of your life and always plays the helpless victim, that is an example of this type of relationship. Victims take on the role of the victimizer, draining you of the resources you require. If you are careless, they will eventually remove all signs of life from you. Victimizers have the potential to dominate our life. And when that occurs, you are unable to accomplish your goals because you must care for a highly dependent individual. You should make an effort to end this harmful relationship as soon as feasible rather than clinging on to it. It will be challenging for you to let go of this relationship because you may have put a lot of time and effort into it, but it is preferable to do so as soon as possible.

3. Always be sincere with others.

An authentic guy or woman is to be valued in today's society. People in society need to be authentic if they want to live better lives. It is simple, cunning, and evil to deceive others, yet there are many con artists and liars in the world. Both your reputation and your soul may be harmed by it. Being genuine to yourself and other people is one of the best things you can do for yourself and other people. By doing so, you can live a life that will ultimately offer you more enjoyment and cause less stress. Since others look up to and trust you to accomplish your work the proper way, authenticity is becoming more and more crucial if you want to be a true leader or manager. If you don't do that, they might look for employment elsewhere. The fundamental rule that ought to guide all of this is to live a life without ever compromising your moral convictions.

4. Be present in the moment and live your life accordingly.

People frequently dwell on the distant past and harbour grudges, or they constantly consider the future. These two approaches are both completely ineffective. This is true for our interpersonal connections as well as the need to maintain our attention on the here and now. Being there for a friend right now is the best thing you can do for them. Right now, your friends need you. Your children and your spouse both need you right now. Spending too much time working, browsing the web, or engaging in other activities is a waste of time. Instead, you should value your current relationships and refuse to sacrifice them for anything.

5. Let go of excessive expectations of other people.

Release the heavy expectations you have of other people is another thing you should do. Your friendship or romantic relationship depends on this. You will have a smoother and simpler relationship with whoever if you keep your expectations for the relationship clear and acceptable. The expectations that many people have of their partners, significant others, or friends are unjustified. This will only cause conflict in the relationship and misery. Divorce and breakups may be the worst outcomes of these assumptions. So it's important to keep up excellent relationships with others while letting go of whatever unrealistic expectations we might have of them.

6. Feel a strong connection with your friend or relationship.

It's vital to go deep in relationships rather than looking for more. You will need to put a lot of time and effort into getting to know someone well. Most of our relationships are only on a surface level, and they end when the other person leaves our lives. It can be because they move away from us or that something at work changes. A major indicator of a genuine relationship with someone else should be their permanence. Do you chat to your friend mostly about sports, Netflix, or other trivial topics, or do you spend more time discussing deeper and more philosophical issues? It is worthwhile to learn more about how to devote more time to the more meaningful aspects of life rather than wallowing in the trivial matters that have no real significance. You may connect with others on a deeper level by going deep.

7. Pay attention to shared experiences.

We are able to create lifelong memories through spending time with friends, family, and other people in our lives. By maximising your time together, you can produce priceless memories. Such memories will last a long time in your heart and thoughts. These memories are more significant than the things we own. They will direct us toward a deeper part of ourselves that we can share.

8. Willfulness.

Intentionality is a crucial component in building healthy connections. When you are deliberate about your relationships, you may communicate more easily and effectively, which will improve the start of your relationships. Spending time with your buddy or partner should have a goal if you want to use it to help you move in the right direction. Your love, romantic, and familial connections will all be enhanced by intentionality.

9. Show neighbourly respect.

Love is the path of pursuing a genuine connection with another person. This is not the kind of sensual love that we typically imagine. Instead, it is a globally applicable idea of human love. How one might have a more meaningful life is defined by their affection for a brother or neighbour. All of your encounters with other people should be infused with love. Because your connection is defined by what you can give to the relationship rather than what you can gain from it, it also makes things a lot prettier and less chaotic. Because of this, it is a less demanding sort of relationship.

10. Embrace connections passionately.

We must pursue our relationships with passion as a final aim. We must not accept anything less than excellence. Relationships take commitment and perseverance to pursue. Because they are fearful or too busy, many individuals don't like to commit to anything. However, you may stand out from the herd and make a commitment to a relationship, whether it be with a friend or a significant other. So look for ways to add some flavour to your life by surrounding yourself with beautiful individuals who will benefit you and who can guide you toward success in life.

Your residence, your online activities, and you

After looking at the advantages of decluttering your home, let's brainstorm some original ways to do it. You may start organising your home by following these straightforward but helpful steps.

Choose the room in the house where you wish to start the decluttering process.

This is the first and most important action you should do. The entire house can't be decluttered in a single day. Even you do, by which we mean you abandoning your daily responsibilities at job, school, or the important assignment you were expected to complete. If you think you can declutter your home in a day, especially if it's your first time, it might be really stressful. You must choose where to start your decluttering because it can take a lot of time. Your bedroom, bathroom, kitchen, living room, dining area, or even the garage could be the location. So that you won't tyre out quickly, start with the easiest one. Then go on to rougher terrain. It's time to move on to the following item on this list once you've decided which location to purge the clutter from.

Set aside 5 to 10 minutes for decluttering.

The process of decluttering is gradual. a procedure you shouldn't haste. You can set aside 5 or 10 minutes each day to organise your home. Increase the duration as you go along and add more things to your list. The first day, for instance, can last 5 minutes. The third could be 15, the fourth could be 10, and so on. Don't spend 10 minutes on decluttering on day one and 5 minutes on day two. Simply put, it won't work. Before you know it, it's difficult for you to set aside even a short period of time to organise your home. Start with the shortest time (5 minutes at the very least) and work your way up.

Obtain a garbage bag.

Get rid of anything that is contributing to the clutter in your home. Grab a garbage bag and place them inside. Give old stuff to a charity if you don't want to get rid of them. Get big boxes if you're planning to store anything. Make room in your home by moving them where they belong. The quantity of trash bags you have removed will astound you.

Make a to-do list of the things you want to discard.

There will undoubtedly be a sizable number of stuff in trash bags that you want to discard. Get a piece of paper, and list everything you wish to get rid of. Cross off each item on your list when you dispose of it. Additionally, it's crucial that you make a to-do list of all your chores so that you may mark off each one as completed. Each item you get rid of helps to clear up the clutter. You can keep track of the jobs you have finished and the ones you haven't by making these lists. If you know where to start and how, decluttering will be simpler.

Make it a goal to discard one item each day.

Try to at least remove one unnecessary thing from your home every day that you chose to clutter it. How about if you did this for a month? 30 things total. If you repeat this process for a year, you must get rid of 365 items. Why don't you make it 2 items per day instead? You'll be able to quickly organise your home and get those things thrown out. Your house will continue to be spotless and dust-free.

Cleaning the house is the same way. most employees with 9 to 5 jobs often struggle to thoroughly clean the entire house, which is quite understandable. You'll need time for it. Start with cleaning one area of your home if you are unable to clean the entire thing. Simply decide to only clean your living room that day and move on to another room the next. Setting and sticking with a goal is what's most crucial.

Take a picture

Although not necessary, this is quite beneficial. You may choose to snap a photo of a messy space, such as your kitchen, and then another photo of the same space. One that's less congested this time. You can see how pleased you have gotten that you have started the process of decluttering your home by looking at those images.

Utilize the four-box method.

Having a strategy in place will make decluttering your home easier than not having one. One of these strategies that will increase your efficiency in cleaning your house is the four-box system. Obtain four boxes, then label each one with the following information:

- Give away: These are boxes that should be stuffed with items that are still fine but that you don't need or use. In other words, these are things that you may either contribute to charitable organisations or sell online.

- Items that you intend to keep should be placed in these boxes. You simply cannot live without them. These are the things you frequently utilise. These include things like your clothes, your stereo system, your chairs, etc. The majority of them are preserved in a set location.
- Things that are lost in your home should be kept in this box, so return. You shouldn't, for instance, have your soap in the living room. You shouldn't have your cutlery in the restroom, etc. The proper places for these goods should be kept there, not the other way around.
- Trash: Place useless items or possessions in this container.

You should put certain goods in the boxes designated for them in each room you enter. No matter how big or small an object is, it should go in the right box. It might take some time, but it will be worthwhile. You will find things and understand what to do with them.

Never be embarrassed to ask for help.

Asking a friend or family member for advice on how to declutter your home is a nice approach to receive it. Your friend or relative can go over all the objects in your home and make recommendations regarding which ones should be donated, given away, or kept. It's completely OK to defend your decision to maintain such a thing. Your choice is sound if your buddy or relative shares your reasoning. If not, it would be best to get rid of the item.

The best part of this is that your friend or family member doesn't have to be an expert to assist you in getting rid of any clutter. Simply put, getting rid of some stuff that you are unsure about getting rid of will be simpler and faster for you if you have someone by your side the entire decluttering process.

Chapter 4: Relationships Decluttering Techniques

The Effects of Poor Relationships

The first step in leaving any toxic relationship is to become aware of the warning flags, acknowledge them, and accept them as facts that are harmful to your wellbeing and need to be changed. Although every person's relationships are unique, here is a closer look at some of the most typical indicators of toxic relationships:

- One indication of a toxic relationship or connection is the use of emotional manipulation.
- Because it can encompass a wide range of acts and behaviours that differ from instance to case, the definition of this symptom varies.
- However, at its foundation, emotional manipulation refers to the purposeful modification of actions or language in order to suppress or control another person's feelings.
- When a toxic individual is present, this can refer to a purposeful escalation of heated feelings and reactions during a conversation with a friend or partner in an effort to persuade them to leave the room or feel helpless in the present circumstance.
- In the victim's situation, they purposefully look for something to do in a different room to avoid

talking to their friend or partner until they are in a better frame of mind since they know that while they are in this state, their tense emotions would only intensify if they try to talk to them.

- severing ties to close family or friends in order to spend more time with a harmful acquaintance or relationship
- In many instances, their friends and family have challenged them about how their loved one has changed in this relationship or connection, which is directly related to and sometimes even the cause of their isolation.
- The person becomes defensive, side with their toxic friend or partner and damaging their relationship with their dependable loved one since they perceive this confrontation as an act of violence.
- anytime you express your views or opinions, you are brushed off as being overly sentimental or overreacting to situations (particularly if they are counter to the toxic friend or partner)
- Sometimes, instead of being ignored, the person is taunted and made fun of, which makes them feel even worse about speaking up.
- If there is a problem the toxic friend or spouse does not want to deal with, they may accuse them of creating difficulties that do not exist. Some toxic

partners may attempt to make the person feel guilty or selfish if their ideas, opinions, or wishes are concentrated on something they need or want.

- Toxic connections and relationships have been linked to a variety of controlling behaviours.
- Sarcastic language and calling someone names in circumstances where it is offensive or hurtful
- Constant, hurtful criticism aimed at undermining their confidence and self-esteem in order to make them easier to manage and control
- when the person becomes too daring or inquisitive for their taste, using coercion and fear techniques
- Making unfounded accusations in an effort to make their spouse feel guilty about something that may not even have happened and blaming the other person for things they had no control over or were even connected to

Whatever their individual characteristics, toxic people have a negative impact on both men and women, regardless of their age or line of work. The more harmful influences there are on a person, the longer or closer their relationship with them is, and the more toxic people there are in the environment. These relationships might be some of the hardest to escape from because they are frequently abusive and even dangerous.

Get rid of bad influences

If you want to genuinely overcome your negative self-talk, you must understand where it originates. People in our immediate surroundings frequently influence the things we think or believe to be true. Our feeling of self-worth can be negatively impacted by even seemingly unimportant or subtly critical remarks or criticism. Our inner voice of critical self-talk stealthily and sneakily transforms into the speech of others. Never let someone else's opinion of you define who you are or serve as the basis for negative self-talk.

Are there people around you who mostly see the negative aspects of your life or theirs? Are you someone else's unwilling victim of their negativity? While it is typical for us to engage in negative self-talk, it is frequently a result of conditioning or the ideas, behaviours, or words of others around us. Dealing with negative criticism that stems from someone else's lack of confidence or self-esteem is extremely difficult. To shift your perspective on life and see it more positively and constructively, go far away from such harmful and negative people.

Be careful not to fall into the trap of negativity set up by others. Avoid spending time with people who constantly complain and whine. Don't join in or act as a willing party to support the complaints of others. A study from the Warsaw School of Social Psychology found that persons who are always complaining have poorer moods, more negative emotions, and less life satisfaction.

Conclusion

We've covered a lot of ground that can help you clear your head and create a new version of yourself. What successful people do to keep their minds on their objectives is covered in the issues we discussed. If you put what is described in this book into practise, you'll discover that nothing you aspire for is out of your reach.

The key to using your mind's power effectively is to act correctly repeatedly rather than just once.

CPSIA information can be obtained
at www.ICGtesting.com
Printed in the USA
LVHW081252101122
732762LV00014B/897

9 780944 251126